In Training: Days of Laughter, Years of Pain

Joan Luckmann

Published by Wayne Luckmann, 2023.

While every precaution has been taken in the preparation of this book, the publisher assumes no responsibility for errors or omissions, or for damages resulting from the use of the information contained herein.

IN TRAINING: DAYS OF LAUGHTER, YEARS OF PAIN

First edition. April 16, 2023.

Copyright © 2023 Joan Luckmann.

ISBN: 979-8215815786

Written by Joan Luckmann.

PROLOGUE [1]

For most of my young life I was known as Ramona Romero until I was 18 years old when I assumed the name of Joan Grey. I decided I could carry two names because I already had lived two entirely different lives that were closely joined. My entire family was odd in that everyone because of their professions had at least two names and often lived double lives. During my early years, my family composed of a crazy cast of characters included play and screenwriters, actors, musicians, as well as faith healers, preachers, and nurses. And because I was part of a theatrical family and I had hoped to follow in their footsteps, I never imagined that someday I would be preparing to become a nurse by entering the notorious Los Angeles County General Hospital, the largest public hospital in the world under one roof at that time with its school for training nurses.

Uncle Ned, a former jazz pianist, former composer, and former drunk, then for several years a sober man who had a fishing tackle business, used to say,

"Ramona, you're going to grow up to be the only normal person in our family."

How wrong he turned out to be! I now surmise that the family heritage carried not only artistic talent but also that of angels and demons dominating our lives and guiding our spirits through the innumerable trials and tribulations, pleasures and pains that we each endured as we struggled our way through our lives.

"Unc", as I used to call him, was handsome, a wonderful pianist and composer, had a great sense of humor, and was hard working when he was sober. He was sober through most of my training, and then tragically, he started drinking again due to some terrible problems with Aunt Margie (his wife). One time when I was a Senior and visiting him on the Violent Men Ward when he was suffering from DTs, witnessing him in such a derelict condition made me aware of how big a role he had played in my life, the only person who had encouraged me to go into training at County because nursing would give me the security of a profession for life.

I had an unusual childhood due to my growing up in the make-believe world of movies, a sad adolescence because of my mother's death and the temporary loss of my dad, those years difficult because of my living with my grandmother Babu when with my mother's death, my entire view of the purpose of my life changed, and I no longer dreamed of being a star in Hollywood or a concert pianist or a person with fame and money. I quit Hollywood Professional School and never touched the piano again. I became obsessed with the lives of the saints, particularly Joan of Arc who became my patron saint, and I went so far as to stop using my birth name Ramona Romero and assumed the name Joan Grey, "Joan" for Joan of Arc, "Grey" in memory of my mother Gloria, a change that when he finally learned of it hurt my father. By studying the lives of saints, I naively thought I would somehow achieve some small measure of their faith, courage, and spiritual stature, and I started thinking about becoming a nurse as a step I thought would lead me toward my goal. I began reading books with titles like *Sue Barton, Student Nurse* and thought less about the saints and more about the science of medicine, less about prayer and more about action, less about caring and more about healing. And once I went into training, instead of reading about the victories of Joan of Arc, the thought of saints disappeared entirely. I concentrated instead on learning anatomy and physiology, nursing arts, surgical techniques, and psychology. The saints had served their purpose and kept me alive and almost sane during a time in my life when suicide seemed not only possible but likely under the naïve idea that I would somehow be reunited with my mother.

Babu, of course, knew nursing, how physically hard and how emotionally crushing it could become. And Babu, whatever her faults, was a good nurse. I remember the patients she took care of in our home and how she never asked for money if she knew they didn't have any. I recall the many "sick calls" we made to patients and how my grandmother truly had a healing touch. At times I disliked her because she was so demanding and always critical of me. The biggest problem for her was that I looked like my dad whom she loathed and not my mother, Gloria Grey, the successful film star. Disliking me because she hated my dad and I looked like him, she always wondering outloud why didn't I look like my mother, how unfair that I grew up feeling there was something wrong with me when she was the chief source of my problems. Yet Babu could not fully destroy my self-esteem because my mother and father had instilled in me a great deal of self-confidence. In their eyes I could do no wrong and would always come out on top.

But when Mother died and Dad had left, I was alone with my grandmother whom I had to fight continuously to hold onto my self-esteem. Even a worse problem, my mother left me defenseless against a woman who was domineering and possessive. Babu tried holding onto everyone she knew, especially Mother, Uncle Ned, Aunt Jessie, and me even though she disliked me and wanted to get rid of me while also refusing to let me go. So during my teens after Mother died, I felt as if I were in a cage until I left for County. Regarding Babu, I used to think, 'You're the one who is trying to destroy me! But I won't let you! I'm going to leave this house as soon as I can!' And when I finally turned 18, I did leave by enrolling in the school of nursing at County, as hard a place to deal with as Babu's house but at least a place where I felt free from her constant condemnation of me and my dad even though I was still angry because I felt my father had deserted me when Mother died, and for a while I grew to dislike him as much as my grandmother.

One day, standing on a street corner in Hollywood, I saw my father not ten feet away. He was looking lovingly at his dog. I thought perhaps I should I say, "Hi, Dad. How have you been? Long time no see!" Instead, I just walked away. Dad never saw me and I never did tell him how close we had been to a possible reunion or more likely a bitter quarrel. I'll never know what might have occurred, but I still think about our accidental meeting that never actually happened. When we eventually did reunite, we did so mostly on his terms after my having repeatedly tried contacting him and finally sought him out in his sanctuary in the Hollywood Hills Yet, neither Uncle Ned nor I could envision the night before I left to start the three years of training that lay ahead at County, but I could recall all too clearly the difficult years that lay behind: the death of my mother from tuberculosis, the disappearance of my father, and the hellish but character building years I spent with Babu, my maternal grandmother, who raised me or rather dragged me up reluctantly through my teens.

But although my family was always an unusual challenge, it was only a prelude preparing me for the challenge that lay ahead at County and the multitude of patients, so many who were homeless, friendless, without family, without hope, in pain and despair we young students were being trained to nurse and ease their suffering in anyway we could, that challenge eventually causing some of us to gradually lose some of our empathy in exchange for our own survival in a brutal world for which we were not ready and often unable to face or accept. For we soon learned that the brutality of life extended far beyond County into the pot-hole streets, rundown houses, and abandoned stores that were the dark poverty filling the heart of East L.A. in such sharp contrast to the world I had lived in my entire life: A beautiful Dutch Colonial house on Crenshaw Boulevard close to Beverly Hills, Bel Air, and the vast, blue ocean with its bright beaches that we could drive to in twenty minutes on what were called freeways, the house I lived in on the border of Hollywood and its own brand of crazy, vivid contrasts from movie star mansions and movie studios and people from all over the world living on the streets, many of them very young, all waiting for that big break, waiting to be discovered, waiting for the fulfillment of that big dream that always remained just a dream.

Yet there also was, of course, the world at large filled with the fear of Communism, filled with prejudice resulting in anger from people of African heritage, Latinos, and Jews; women with no legal rights; few with little more than basic schooling or wealth; homosexuals locked in a dark closet; all these bitter people forced to live on the fringes of society waiting for their time to emerge into the light while others formed grandiose plans to make their way off of our chaotic world and soar through the heavens to the moon and eventually the stars.

Having said all that, now I should begin my story and my last night with Babu before I left the next day for my three years at Los Angeles County General Hospital School of Nursing.

September 8, 1954: I begin my new life

Temperatures already in the mid-sixties promising another hot, smoggy, September day in Los Angeles and I am preparing myself to face three years at Los Angeles County General Hospital. I had heard it referred to as "The Rock" or "The Great Stone Mother." If that wasn't enough to scare me, I had also heard rumors that if you could survive at County, you could survive just about any problem life hurled your way, but I already had enough problems I was attempting to survive. Trying to finish packing my bags in what had once been my mother's bedroom before she died, this day for me is special, an exciting day, a liberating day because today I am finally leaving my grandmother's house. I am finally leaving a place where I had grown through childhood, the only place I'd ever lived, leaving behind memories that I wanted to preserve as well as too many memories I wanted to forget. Most important of all, on this day, at long last, I am leaving Babu, my grandmother who raised me after my mother died seven years earlier.

Only five feet tall, but strong and sturdy, built like a Slavic peasant who has labored in the fields her whole life and has known nothing but hardship, with her dark blue eyes and her graying hair wrapped around her head in a tight braid, Babu is a powerful woman. Commanding, domineering, possessive, my grandmother is someone I am compelled to respect but can never love. Babu always an enigma, living with her has always been difficult. She could be decent, reasonable, and fair eighty percent of the time, but that other twenty percent of the time was cruel and often seemed fatal, so that twenty percent of abuse is what I remember most. All the good works my grandmother performed by helping others were negated by what she created with her anger at anyone whom she thought reduced her feelings of power and self-respect or anyone who stood in her way of possessing the people in her life she wanted to control.

I wrestled with those problems for all the years I knew her, but when I finally left I only found myself in a place even more harsh and more demanding where I was challenged by someone with even more power over me, someone who apparently believed that she, too, was helping me and others with her facile, destructive form of counseling. But, just like Babu, she too often exerting her power over us, reduced some students to the brink of tears and others even to the brink of psychic collapse. I eventually got away from her, too, but before I did, I would have to gather my strength to not let anyone control my thoughts and make me doubt myself by thinking I was in constant denial because I was too afraid to face the problems from my past mostly due to my grandmother.

Babu a beautiful woman had passed that quality to her daughter Gloria Grey who until she became ill was successful in both silent and talking films. [2]

I always had a portrait photo of Mother on my dresser prompting curious people to ask why I had a framed photo of a movie star so prominently displayed.

For some reason typical of her, Babu had our portrait photographs taken shortly after Mother died. I, of course, look totally in despair while my grandmother manages to still look proud and stoic even though I knew her heart was breaking. She should have been more angry with my mother's Christian Science counselor who had insisted that Mother keep her faith strong and refuse any medication or drugs, but so great was Babu's sorrow she couldn't spare the energy to hate him, nor did she have the emotional strength to seek legal charges against him for his total disregard of my mother's life when newly approved medications were available that could have saved her.

With her blue eyes and white hair, Babu a powerful woman, short, sturdy, proud, she was always the center of attention, as Dr. Grey, Mother Grey, always a contradiction, the sort of person you admired yet disliked, when Babu declared:

"If it's a choice between having love or respect, I want respect!" And you better believe she got it!

A portrait photo of Babu I once had displays her in a white nurse's uniform with white hair in tight braids on top of her head held high, proud, almost arrogant. Another photograph of Babu displays her in a long striped apron over her long, white, starched uniform, her beautiful long auburn hair swept up into a bun on top of her head, she holding my mother in her arms at whom she was smiling sweetly.

Sometimes a savior, sometimes a villain, never a friend, far too harsh and unpredictable, her major problem: she was so volatile. Something you thought she would surely be angry about she willingly accepted. Something minor and she would explode. So what made Babu so difficult to deal with was her bi-polar, manic-depressive personality that made her so unpredictable. I would have found much easier dealing with someone always mean with an obvious cruel streak always present who didn't care about anyone, never did anything without expecting payment, always forgetting any wrong she, herself, might have done, always walking over people using them as stepping stones to get to what she wanted. I found so much simpler and easier just outright hating someone with all my being, despising everything she did as a constant source of abuse and pain and get away from her, even perhaps killing her and ridding the world of such an ogre.

But my problem arose when a person like Babu could be abusive, possessive, and hateful one minute and then suddenly become kind and understanding although still possessive, the bonds she tied never loosened but tightened until I nor anyone could get away from her whenever her mood suddenly changed. The fact Babu was so unpredictable, so changeable, so erratic in addition to the loss of my mother and disappearance of my father caused me continual grief. I was always torn between feeling hateful toward her or feeling guilty about my hateful thoughts. I became as changeable as she, never knowing how to act, never knowing what to expect, my life built around a rotating wheel of fortune that sometimes spun fast and furious in the wind and at other times turned quietly in a soft breeze. I never knew for one moment to the next what she would do and why I wanted to just hate her, something I just couldn't do.

Babu's greatest fault was her having driven out of her life the people she loved most because of her need to possess them. But I think she could not keep herself from acting that way toward others. Babu could be a bully, and she was often frightening because she was very unpredictable. Yet although Babu could be a bully herself, she would not allow anyone to bully another person. She would defend someone no matter what that person had done, as she did Rosemary abused by her father for becoming pregnant. But only one singular time did she accord with me and my father in condemning Christian Science by supporting our opposition to my mother's strict adherence to a faith that led to her early death from tuberculosis that could have been prevented had she agreed to take newly introduced drugs.

Most other times, Babu always felt she was always right and always doing the right thing for other people. I don't know if she understood how her possessiveness affected others in unsurprising and very negative ways. I think Babu saw her possessiveness as a form of protecting others, although at some level she must have understood that she was destroying lives and that she had definitely destroyed my mother's marriage.

My grandmother also lived with pride from my mother's success. Mother would have been even more successful as an actress if she hadn't gotten ill. And while Babu loved attention and drama that focused on her, Mother's death definitely shocked her and eventually contributed to her own demise from a final stroke.

Babu stands in the doorway of my bedroom watching me with a spiteful look while I go on packing trying to ignore her study of my every move.

"Nursing is hard, dirty work," she again warns quietly. "You won't be able to take it."

Then suddenly pointing her finger at me, she raises her voice to a shout as if she were preaching one of her Sunday sermons:

"Mark my words, you'll be back!"

Preaching on Sundays, Babu always wore her long, white dress trimmed in dazzling gold with what seemed a gold halo around her head, her arms stretched out to beckon lost wanderers to join her flock. People once said that Babu was a lot like Amy Semple McPherson, a famous preacher at the time. If Babu had not been so burdened with my mother, my alcoholic uncle Ned, and me, she probably would have become as famous as any preacher of that era

Her pale white skin making Babu very vain, she knew how to put on a dramatic performance anywhere, anytime. She could have been in movies along with my mother. Her sense of drama made Babu an inspirational preacher, for she knew how to lower and soften her voice when speaking to her followers often lolling them to sleep then almost screaming at them – poor timid sheep – to wake them up.

Aunt Jessie and I often sat in Mother's old study right behind the living room wall and listened to Babu's weekly Sunday sermon, she always wearing that long white silk robe, with her white braids, pale skin enhancing her mannerisms, Babu appeared as holy as an angel or a saint. Her flock totally believed in her in every way, and since she had done something kind and helpful for everyone of them, they all loved her without reservation.

If Babu were alive today, she would probably become our first woman president, for Babu had every requirement to rise in politics: strength, ruthlessness, a willingness to present herself as always confident, mightier than she actually was, a way with people that made them feel important, the ability to move people so that they felt she was actually doing something for them rather than just for herself in order for her to maintain her power to promote her own, self-righteous beliefs and her goal of always seeking more wealth and usually succeeding by exploiting others.

Babu producing troubled relationships by always trying to dominate others was rarely if ever a victim herself, and Babu seemed remarkably lacking in prejudice against anyone, except my father. She was very upset when our Japanese gardener and his family were sent to a concentration camp in 1941. We for awhile also had a black live-in maid. One day when I was a child, I got angry because I was denied something I desperately (and selfishly) wanted and called Gertrude a nasty name. Babu was furious and loudly ordered me to tell Gertrude I was sorry. I really did feel sorry because I saw how Gertrude was so hurt when she had always been kind and helpful to me. She kindly forgave my childish rant, and I never labeled anyone with that odious word again.

Aunt Jessie, her closest friend with whom she continually fought, always said that because Babu had grown up alone in an orphanage and with no one who wanted her or cared about her compelled her to cling to those whom she considered her family because never having had her own she needed them so desperately.

I try to ignore her and continue packing, but I can't shut out her words. Babu loves drama, and I always have been her captive audience. I think about leaving the room, but that wouldn't help because she will just follow me, so I brace myself to listen to her usual tirade for what seems like the thousandth time. I have heard Babu spit out these same words over and over for years in her usual tirade. Babu steps close to me and points her finger at me.

"I don't get one ounce of gratitude from you — not one ounce — after all I've done for you!"

My grandmother moves even closer. I can smell the sweet scent of the soap that she always uses.

"I've worked my fingers raw and bleeding to keep a roof over your head and food on the table! I could have let your selfish father have custody, but I saved you from the miserable gypsy life you would have had with him. And you! You're never grateful! Not one word of thanks do I get from you!"

I give up trying to pack and flee into the spacious living room, but she follows.

"I give you one month!" she shouts, "and then, believe me, you will be back!"

I finally turn to face her. "No I won't!" I cry. "The hospital may be as bad as it is here, but at least it will be different!" Little did I know then that the difference would be worse.

I flee the house into the beautiful backyard that Babu has nourished with her green thumb where she also built a barbeque pit, hauling in alone brick and heavy bags of cement for a patio she laid herself. Babu has such a green thumb everything she touches grows in abundance. Plants so love her, she can grow anything even in poor soil, summer or winter. We have a beautiful rose garden in back, a arbor of dark grapes over the back porch, a rose arbor at the entrance in front, an expansive lawn back and front always green. For awhile she had a fern bed and planted hibiscus. Mother and I would string the petals into leis. Babu also planted a jungle in the backyard with a trail that my only friend Paula and I tramped through on our adventures. We thought we could make tires from rubber trees and put them on trains and go all over the country.

[Paula Strahm by email recalls: "The 'jungle' was part of our 'Locket' script [for] dual ad-lib imaginary playing as children with no props of any kind, just the imagination of two young girls who wanted to conquer other worlds and make them better. We wanted to get back to New York where Joan's mother had been for a while where she met Ramona's father Ramon Romero, another extraordinary person."]

Yet living with Babu has always been hard because Babu had an equally hard life. Babu had no relatives other than immediate family. Raised in an orphanage, becoming a nurse when nurses mostly scrubbed floors, seeing my mother die, and then having to raise me on top of everything else, especially as I looked so much like my father, and oh, how she hated him, I felt she hated me.

Babu always claimed to have been born in Wales, another fabulation on her part. She just wanted to appear more exotic to others. Babu actually born in Oregon of Slavic heritage soon after became an orphan when her mother died and her father left Babu in a Catholic orphanage but said that he would someday come back to get her from that horrible place. From her account, Babu's childhood in that orphanage was terrible. She claimed the nuns were mean and always beating her for any infraction however minor, they having been forced as young girls into a convent to live a life demanded of them by their parents and their faith. My mother and I knew Babu had to believe her father loved her and did not desert her. But he never came back, and Babu was adopted when she was about eleven or twelve by a family apparently very kind to her, giving her a decent home until she was fourteen or fifteen when they helped Babu enter training to become a nurse and become emancipated. Babu graduated from nursing school, became an RN, and later developed skills in physical therapy.

Babu would never admit that her father had abandoned her. She always claimed he was a war hero greatly decorated from not caring if he died because he wanted to be with his wife in heaven. I know he was a decorated soldier because I saw his photo that Babu always carried with her. But if he had been a real hero, surely he wouldn't have left his child in an orphanage.

Babu so very possessive and controlling, she didn't want me leaving, especially since she knew I was determined to leave anyway, for I saw both the good and the bad in her and I grew up fearing her, especially after my mother died. Mother had protected me from my grandmother's bi-polar personality, and once Mother was gone, my grandmother was free to treat me any way she wanted on any given day depending on her mood, so I never knew what to expect, and I came to expect the worse.

Yet no matter how I felt about my grandmother, most people adored her. To her clients, Babu was almost a saint, and I believe that she really did care about the people she treated, for she never charged a client if she knew that the client or the client's family was poor. Men resented Babu but respected her. They paid her the greatest compliment any woman could hope to hear at the time: "She thinks like a man."

Babu did think like a shrewd business woman and always was a tough opponent, but Babu never truly loved any man, apparently not even Mr. Grey. She always had harsh words for him even when they were a young couple. Babu used to love telling the story of when Mr. Grey was working in a rather lowly position at a bank. One day they were in the kitchen where Babu was fixing scrambled eggs and my grandfather was reading the paper. Babu suddenly picked up the frying pan, aimed it directly at my poor grandfather and, as she said, "I just let it fly!" hitting Mr. Grey on the side of his head, creating a nasty wound and a burn from the hot butter and eggs that had splattered all over him. My grandfather was so shocked he couldn't even respond. Babu shook a large spatula at him and yelled,

"God damn you! We don't have a thing! This little house! No furniture! Hardly any decent food! You quit that job at the bank and get a good job! One that really pays! One that will make us rich!"

I don't know what Mr. Grey might have said. Most likely nothing, as he usually did in response to Babu's tirades, but I learned that he had quit the bank, went into real estate buying property at twenty dollars an acre in the desert, and became a partner in one of the companies starting a little desert community called Palm Springs. Of course, Mr. Grey grew wealthy, and Babu always took the credit. In time, he made more money than she did, so Babu even though she had divorced him wanted some of what he had gained, and however much she might have received, she would have taken it all had she somehow managed, and I think he probably did give her some because Mr. Grey was somewhat afraid of her, especially after the abuse he took from her early in their marriage.

Other men often viewed Babu as a powerful woman, a view not readily accepted at the time, and I don't recall any men attending her Sunday sermons or any male clients in her therapy practice while women always held Babu in awe as someone progressive. Very few women in that era could achieve what Babu accomplished with little help from anyone while facing all the problems she had to endure surviving adoption, training to be a nurse, marriage to her Swedish husband, having my mother, married to Mr. Grey, having my uncle, starting her own nursing and physical therapy practice, founding an apostolic church, caring for my uncle when he was recovering from an accident driving while drunk, raising me, caring for my mother while watching her die. Babu's hardships as a child and a young student nurse had left her with a taint of arrogance, she always having something to prove and usually gaining anything she wanted because Babu knew how to intimidate people, especially me.

So possessive and controlling, she didn't want me leaving her house especially when she knew I was leaving despite whatever she said however loud. Yet finally she leaves me alone, apparently to allow me to reconsider what she has advised, but I only think of her harangue that occurred the evening before when I reluctantly went back into the house from the garden in back after Aunt Jessie had called me to dinner of another great meal by Babu always the great cook including roast lamb, mashed potatoes, Babu's canned peas, freshly baked apple pie I shared with Babu, Jessie, and Johnnie in our beautiful dining room beyond the blue and white Dutch kitchen.

Jessie and Johnnie try being nice, encouraging me about what was ahead for me, Babu silently angry, fuming inside.

I excuse myself, "I should do my packing."

Babu stops my flight. "Aren't you going to help with dishes?"

Jessie and Johnnie both respond almost at the same time, "That's OK, Mona. We'll do them."

Babu glares at them more angry than ever.

Babu too often a bully, she frightens me because she is so unpredictable, and she believes in corporal punishment. She adheres to the adage that you must straighten a child before the age of seven or the child will grow up crooked, or some such saying just as harsh that asserts children should be subject to abuse for their own good and hitting or even beating a child is sanctioned by custom. When I did something she thought improper, she would become very threatening. I would beg her to reason about the problem and sometimes she did but sometimes she didn't and she would hit me with a coat hanger, bending it while supposedly straightening me.

Babu follows me into my bedroom once my mother's before her death, Babu forcing me to sleep in the same bed in which my mother died.

"Nursing is hard, dirty work! I should know! I've had to take care of your mother! I have worked my fingers to the bone taking care of you! I've had to be father and mother to you!"

Babu snatches a picture of my father and me out of my hand that I'm about to pack. Her eyes fill with hate.

"He never did anything but control your mother and ruin her life!"

How many times had I heard her accuse Dad of being a Svengali casting a spell, keeping an evil hold on my mother?

Babu hated my coloring always reminding her of my father and his Gypsy heritage. "You're just like your father!"

I still remember my grandmother pulling my hair while brushing and exclaiming: "Why aren't you blond like your mother instead of dark like your father!" Although an early photos depicts me as having light brown hair.

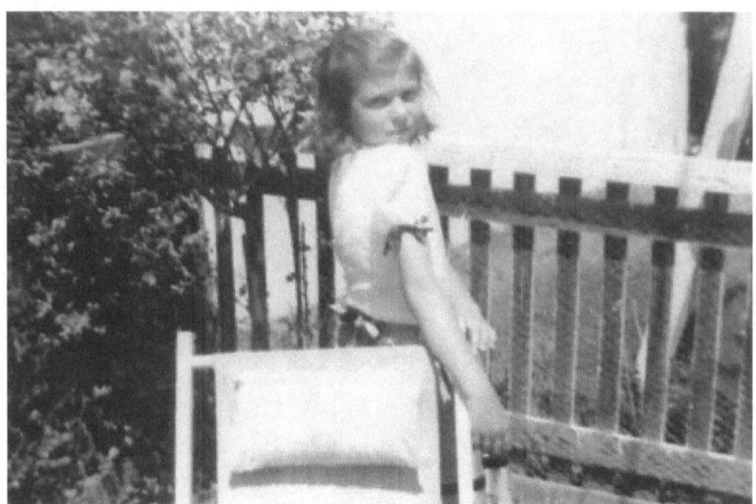

Babu hates everything about my father, but she actually is the problem: Possessive with everyone – Mother, me, Aunt Jessie — Babu is jealous because she suspects something she can't accept is going on between Jessie and Johnnie who had lived together before moving in with Babu when Babu had immediately claimed Jessie as her own.

According to Jessie, the three of them had fought every night for ten years. One night Babu woke me, got me out of bed, told me to get dressed, and said that we were leaving. I never understood where we were going as Babu could not drive! So we stood outside for a while on the front lawn then went back into the house and I went back to bed. What that was all about I'll never know, most likely the result of one of those nightly fights among the three women that lasted until Babu grew seriously ill.

Babu thrusts at me another photo that includes my father.

"Here, take it! Take this one too!"

From that picture of my mother, my dad, and me, Babu has cut out the image of my father! I am stunned. I am so glad that I am leaving here and leaving her. What am I supposed to do with this mutilated picture?

"As far as the training you'll get, you won't be able to stand it! You'll be back, Mona! Believe me!"

I tell myself: "Never! I'm never coming back! I don't care how bad it is, I'm never coming back!"

Babu finally leaves me alone in my room. Jessie and Johnnie come to hug me and wish me well. Johnnie leaves and Jessie sits on the bed while I continue packing.

I never knew Aunt Jessie's full name. She wasn't my real aunt; she was always just Aunt Jessie to me, my "play" aunt, Babu's best and most likely intimate friend who had a close relationship with Aunt Johnnie, my other play-aunt, always a source of contention with Babu. I had no knowledge of Aunt Jessie's background other than her having been born in St. Louis. I knew nothing of her parents since she never discussed her family, so I never knew whether she had siblings or why she had never married. I knew she had finished high school and trained to be a secretary.

In her 40s, Jessie seemed old, but then everyone at that time looked old to me, although she wasn't overweight like Babu. She was trim and she was taller than my grandmother who was only 5 feet tall. Jessie's clothing style was always conservative, mostly suits and sensible shoes with short heels, mostly because of her employment.

Other than her strikingly blue eyes, Aunt Jessie's appearance was nondescript, very plain looking with brown hair and bangs to cover her high forehead she hated. She wore only a bit of lipstick, and I can't remember much about her appearance except she seemed quiet and humble and sort of blending into the woodwork until I saw her at her office when she was at her job. There she looked very efficient, professional, someone to be respected. She was for years executive secretary for the head of the Santa Fe railroad and looked every bit the part. We used to joke about how she wrote all of the letters for her boss and that she was the one actually running the company, her writing the CEO's letters and memos probably the main reason the railroad was still running and not in some giant train wreak at the bottom of a canyon.

Always serious, Aunt Jessie read the daily newspaper she considered the poor person's encyclopedia, but she read few books, and although she did not read widely, she always seemed well-informed and wise. Aunt Jessie was the picture most people have of a typical old maid, the most patient person I've ever met, especially with me. Aunt Jessie used to sit in a special, very comfortable chair after dinner and I'd sit on the floor and we'd talk, I mostly complaining about how difficult Babu was and how I wished she would change for the better, and Aunt Jessie quietly, patiently listening to my too often repeated tale of woe.

Just the opposite of Babu, she was almost impossible to shake or upset. She didn't have any disabilities, was always in excellent health, and I can't recall her ever being sick. She also seemed totally lacking in any sexuality. I can't image Aunt Jessie involved with a man although I think she would have made a wonderful mother.

Jessie and Babu and Johnnie fought continually at night for ten years, about what I never did know, but I suspect that Babu was very jealous of Johnnie because Babu wanted Aunt Jessie all to herself. Babu was jealous of Jessie's close friendship with Aunt Johnnie with whom she had lived before both came to live with Babu. What made the friendship among the three even more curious was that although Johnnie and Jessie had a close relationship, to everyone's surprise, especially mine, Johnnie for a time suddenly became engaged to a nice looking man, and Eric and Johnnie would put on quite a show for me at night when I looked out my window and could see them kissing. I don't know if Johnnie was ever serious about getting married to a man since Eric and Johnnie broke their brief engagement and I never did find out why or whatever happened to Eric. My feeling was that Johnnie was never interested in men, but she thought she would give it a try, and when it didn't work out, Aunt Jessie, Johnnie, and Babu were back to their nightly fights. Fortunately, no one used alcohol or they probably would have killed each other.

This morning after breakfast, I'm back in my bedroom trying to finish packing to leave Babu and start training. I'm waiting for Aunt Jessie to take me to County. For what she knows is the last time, Babu tries to keep me from going. She as usual is raging at me. I'm trying to get away from her by fleeing into the living room, the kitchen, her treatment room, but she follows me continuing to yell. When I don't respond, Babu finally understands that I'm leaving despite anything she says.

I keep wondering where is Aunt Jessie? Please come so I can get out of here! But when I move through the house one last time, I see again how beautiful it is: My mother's room, small but quite fancy with a pink satin quilted bedspread, mostly as it was when she lived but changed only because it was now mine; the gorgeous living room with sofa and matching chairs with printed gold fabric of large oriental designs; the big Dutch kitchen with blue and white cabinets and checkered tile floor; the beautiful rose garden my grandmother had planted along with the rose arbor out front.

I finally sit down on a bench in the hallway by the front door waiting for Aunt Jessie and I consider what I have been through and learned while living in Babu's house: Married to a tall, blonde Swede, Babu had my mother when she was only sixteen or seventeen. My mother seemed to know nothing about her biological father except that he was Swedish. Babu divorced him while Mother was very young and went on to marry Mr. Grey, a Serbian, with whom she had Uncle Ned. I met Mr. Grey many times but I never liked him. Yet since he had made a lot of money in real estate in Palm Springs, Babu always wanted me to be very sweet to Mr. Grey, but I never called him grandfather or grandpa. I could only be polite. I never could accept having to "kiss up" to anyone who had money or something I wanted. I remember that Babu always was irritated because of my unfriendly attitude toward Mr. Grey.

Yet, the only person Babu truly loved was my mother, but in some weird way she must have felt something for Mr. Grey besides anger because she always wanted something from him, something he wouldn't readily give her – his money. I suspect my mother wasn't very close to her stepfather. Mother desperately ill for a long time, I don't remember Mr. Grey ever visiting her. My grandmother divorced him and became very close to Aunt Jessie and Aunt Johnnie. Just before her divorce, Babu went to Hawaii leaving Mr. Grey standing on the dock watching my grandmother sail away with her friends whom she cared for more than him, if she ever actually had cared for him at all.

Babu learned later that he finally did have money that he had earned because of her relentless threats and demands, and she, of course, wanted a share but apparently was denied what she claimed her due reward. As a result, Babu almost lost our house soon after mother died, so she with only required help refurbished our large house into apartment units and afterwards was always able to make the mortgage payments. Babu also had street savvy. An astute business woman, sometimes she seemed a bit of a con reading tea leaves, gazing into crystal balls, using a Ouija board trying to contact "the dearly departed," all for a fee. Kind to patients, devoted to my mother, extremely hard working to a fault, I often found Babu scrubbing the kitchen ceiling shouting, "Cleanliness is next to godliness!" Using her talents in many ways, she was always busy because "idle hands do the Devil's work.

When Babu suffered her first stroke, she continued to work as a physical therapist for a demanding doctor. One day when she couldn't make it up the stairs to his office, he had yelled down at her, "Get up here even if you have to crawl!" Babu did crawl to work that day, but when she established a treatment room in our house she would never again have to endure such insults. Babu had a very successful practice and she also took in patients after surgery.

One time, when I was about 13, we took in an unmarried beautiful German girl who had become pregnant. Her father, a horrible man who beat her, later died of cancer, an end I thought he deserved because I felt that a man so cruel had no right to live. I shared my room with Rosemary and she seemed to have been resigned to her father's frequent abuse, but I often was so upset I was sick to my stomach most of the time she stayed with us. I never knew what happened to the baby, but Rosemary trained to be a nurse and graduated from County, so I admired her and wanted to be like her. Rosemary warned me not to train at County and advised me that I should attend another school for nursing that was easier and less exhausting. She said that the students at County were all young girls who at the end of a day of working the numerous wards on so many of the eighteen floors they would all return to their rooms and go directly to bed. But despite hearing that bad report, I later enrolled in County anyway, mostly to get away from Babu but also because of my fondness and respect for Rosemary.

Babu loved to gamble, especially playing bingo and some strange game where everyone threw balls in the center of the gambling hall. Babu always said that she liked gambling because she needed to relax after a stressful week, but Babu had never learned to drive, so Aunt Jessie did all the driving, and we always had Chevies, always brown. We used to go out for a long drive every Sunday after my grandmother's sermon, go for dinner to Babu's favorite restaurant for prime rib, then out to Venice where Babu would gamble until eleven at night when we'd go home and Babu and my make-believe aunts would get ready for another day of work and I another day at school. Every Sunday we did the same thing: a long drive, a sumptuous dinner of prime rib at Babu's favorite restaurant, then out to Venice where I waited with Aunt

Jessie outside the gambling hall, or Aunt Jessie would take me out onto the boardwalk to observe all the muscle men displaying their bodies, or we would watch the Fat Lady, a hugh woman who appeared made of rubber as she laughed and laughed and laughed at all of us idiots gawking at her.

We also used to go on longer overnight trips, but I would always get car sick and had to be brought home. We did visit almost every California mission within a day's drive when I was in my phase of reading about the lives of saints, especially about Joan of Arc whom I thought my patron saint and whose name I later assumed as my own when I enrolled in the Los Angeles County General Hospital School of Nursing.

Babu, however, wasn't interested as I was in reading fiction or fantasy, perhaps because she lived it. I never saw her sitting quietly reading a book. She was always up and busy. She painted her kitchen Dutch blue and white with a white ceiling that she scrubbed at least once a week. Always a compulsive cleaner always scrubbing something, she was most interested in and focused on her therapy and home nursing business, her apostolic church, her in-home patients that brought in money, the more the better.

Babu loved crocheting or knitting or weaving large rugs that were beautiful and looked like something you might find in an adobe hut during the early days in the West. Babu loved all colors except black. She wove rugs in multiple colors and we had furniture beautifully coordinated with throws of Chinese patterns in gold cloth that was the fashion at the time. For a while, we had a beautiful home with a spiral staircase until Babu converted her house into apartments, an office, and an exam room for her therapy practice in order to save us from foreclosure. After Babu had another stroke, she needed to work at home and that way she also could keep an ever watchful eye on me. She wanted to build her own church, to make a lot of money, to accumulate property, to help my mother get well, and to keep her family members (especially me) under her control.

Aunt Jessie was Babu's best friend and I know Babu loved Jessie as dearly as I did, but Babu's attitude toward women was ambiguous. While she had two husbands, she had no other male friends, and she seemed so very close to Aunt Jessie, even sharing with her the same bed. If they lived today, they would likely marry.

When Aunt Jessie finally pulls up to the **curb** in our Chevy, I pick up my bags and hurry out through the beautiful rose arbor, the grass lawn beside the walkway neatly trimmed, the whole grand Dutch Colonial inviting and immaculate to anyone who hasn't lived there with Babu.

Babu follows me and now changes her approach becoming nicer. I feel confused. I always feel confused around Babu. You never know what mood she's coming out of or when. Babu doesn't want me leaving her house, especially when she sees I am obviously leaving anyway.

Aunt Jessie helps me lift my bags into the trunk.

"I thought you'd never come!" I whisper with grateful relief.

Always calm, she quietly answers: "Stop worrying, Mona. I'll get you to the hospital in plenty of time. We won't get lost. County is way too big to miss."

Babu stands on the curb resuming her rant about how dangerous East L.A. is with its poverty, gangs, drunks, homeless, and drug addicts. She throws a newspaper at me.

"You don't believe me, Mona! Here, read this! Take it with you! Read it when you get to the hospital! By then it will be too late!"

I don't respond to her final assault, ignore the newspaper, climb in the Chevy, and wait for Aunt Jessie to take me away leaving Babu behind on the curb watching us go.

Aunt Jessie says she doesn't want to drive the new Pasadena freeway, so we take the alternative old route to the hospital through downtown L.A. and head for State Street and Marengo, the neighborhood, as Babu predicted, growing worse with homeless on sidewalks of downtown Los Angeles and derelict houses as we get closer to the Eastside, a striking contrast to Babu's beautiful home. As we start across the Macy Street Art Deco bridge that marks the border to East L.A., Aunt Jessie exclaims at seeing the hospital even at a distance its massive white bulk soaring above the surrounding plain of houses. [3]

"There it is! I'm glad that you're the one going there and not me. I'd just as soon keep working for the railroad."

"That must be so boring!"

"Well, yes, sometimes it is, and I have to admit sometimes pretty awful too. Especially the kind of jobs they offer women along with the rotten pay. I hope that after your training in that monstrosity you'll at least be able to earn a decent living, if you don't get married to some doctor with money."

"I'm not going to marry for money!" I'm going to make my own money.!"

"Watch out, sweet child. You'll end up an old maid like me."

"I'd rather be an old maid anytime than be some man's slave!"

Aunt Jessie just looks ahead and smiles.

We pass gangs of loitering young Latinos on the streets beneath the monumental grandeur of the hospital that looks like a mighty fortress I've heard called "The Rock," a beacon especially at night to the sick and suffering masses of Latinos and other poor ethnic groups who inhabit East L.A., the hospital also a notorious training ground for those of us who want to learn how to alleviate suffering and ease the pain of dying.

What will those patients be like? Was my grandmother right? Is the task just a challenging, dirty, thankless job as she has so often loudly claimed? Now after an initial sense of relief getting away from my former house and neighborhood, I start to feel anxious, my most common response to anything unknown to me.

The hospital as we get closer looks so hugh, so overwhelming, so frightening that I am becoming scared and want to go back to where conditions were miserable but at least predictable and I knew what to expect. What was it going to be like working inside that massive eighteen-story monster above a cavernous basement rising before me as we slowly approach?

Aunt Jessie smiles. "Getting excited or just getting scared?"

"A little of both. But at least I won't have Babu yelling at me."

"Yes, but you'll have doctors, patients, instructors yelling at you. Someone is always yelling at you in this world, Mona."

"That shouldn't be!"

"Well, dear child, I learned long ago that life isn't easy or what you think it ought to be!" Then she adds, "But at least we have it better than the poor little children in China."

We both laugh.

"Aunt Jessie?" I suddenly ask what I've always wanted to ask. "Why have you stuck with Babu all of these years? She's always trying to pick a fight with you over something stupid! She's always possessive of you and of me, just as she was of my mother! She doesn't want anyone to even breathe without her permission! She wants to keep a strangle hold on all of us! Why do you still put up with all that!"

"I'm your grandmother's friend," Aunt Jessie replies quietly as a matter of fact, "I help her stay stable. Babu has had a hard life abandoned as an infant, growing up in an orphanage, watching your mother die, and then raising you. She didn't have to, you know."

But Aunt Jessie's response only begins to irritate me. "Why do you always defend her!"

"Because I'm her friend – that's what friends do."

"I still don't see why you put up with it!"

But I can see that Aunt Jessie is getting tired of an exchange we must have had too many times. Aunt Jessie closes her lips tightly and looks straight ahead. I know well what that means without her saying a word:

("Shut up, child! I don't want to talk about it anymore!")

Now that we are closer to the hospital and it grows even larger, I'm definitely starting to feel excited. There is something about the place with its giant, towering wings generating an intimidating force emanating from its huge bulk. Here we are before what I have read is the largest public hospital in the world under one roof.

[4]

I ask Aunt Jessie to circle the hospital so I can show her how grand it is and I excitedly point out the magnificent entrance to the hospital with its statues of the founding deities of medicine, Pasteur, Vesalius and Harvey, on one side; Hippocrates, Galan, and Hunter, on the other that stand above the doorway of the Acute Unit above the wide flight of 30 steps with two landings.

[5]

Having seen them in the brochure I received with an application to the nursing school, I with growing excitement point out the major areas as if I already knew the place well: The older Acute unit and more recently completed Psychiatric unit, the older TB and Osteopathic units that look antique compared to the new CD unit. We view people of all ages laboring up the wide stairs of the entrance or limping down. We witness the expressions of sadness, anxiety, anger, pain, or relief on the faces of little children and the elderly perhaps from receiving a recent diagnosis or treatment. We finally pull up to the entrance of a modern brick building two stories high, the new apartment unit for student nurses completed the previous year. [6] [7]

Opposite the brick building across from the psychiatric unit are two-story wood barracks referred as cottages we will live in once we are capped after three or four months of probation, the remaining months as official students until summer vacation when we'll be suddenly reborn as Juniors. There's a big chain-link fence around the barracks.

We pull up behind a line of other cars beside the brick building. Other new students are getting out with their parents, hauling out their luggage, climbing the few wide stairs, and entering the residence. Everyone looks excited but anxious. I feel the same.

"Well, here we are! Let's go!" Aunt Jessie exclaims as she climbs out of the Chevy and opens the trunk. We start unloading my luggage then climb the stairs along with others.

"Yes," I say to myself, "Here we are! Let the games begin!" Little do I know then how soon I will learn what little fun those games will offer.

Aunt Jessie and I enter the foyer. Most new students seem about my age, some shy, some loud, all anxious. Several older women in their twenties seem less nervous, more confident that they are going to make it through this difficult day. A cluster of five men who appear in their mid-twenties, probably medics who served in Korea, a couple look somewhat effeminate, and I recall how people look down on male nurses although they look up to medics as heroes. The male students are introducing themselves to each other and exchanging war stories, real or imagined. They look pretty blasé compared to the rest of us. I'm sure they have seen it all: shattered bones, bloody faces, death and dying. This place may be a stroll in the park for them.

Students seemed to be arriving in shifts. I look around and wonder how many of us will be left by the end of the month. I hope one of them will be me. Aunt Jessie having helped me lug in my bags, gives me a hug and a kiss, and tells me to call my grandmother to let her know that I'm OK.

"Ramona, I know you don't want to call her, but you need to do the right thing!"

Then she leaves, and I watch her descend the stairs to her car. I suddenly feel all alone. Well, I guess I got what I wished for, despite my long-lost father's frequent warning.

Two housemothers check us in, give us our schedules, and take us to our rooms. One of the housemothers seems very nice, but the one who admits me I learn later has been a guard at Tehachapi State Prison for Women, unfriendly, ordering students around as if they were convicts, acting as if she were still a guard. She, of course, is the one who checks me in. Lucky me to be assigned to her!

"State your name! Here, fill out these forms and sign them!"

I find an empty place to sit, fill out the forms and sign them, then take them to the prison guard.

"Pick up your bags, Grey! Follow me!"

So I follow her down the hall to a room with two beds, a chest of drawers, a desk, and two utility chairs. The room looks very modern and what I would expect in a college dorm. I see the magazine *Seventeen* lying on my roommate's bedside table. [8]

"Don't get too used to this," the Tehachapi State Prison guard warns. "Once you get your cap – if you get your cap – you'll be moving into the barracks across the way. We prefer to call them cottages. Not as fancy as this, but they work. Put your bags down, Grey! Keep your schedule for the first week handy! Don't lose it! Be sure you follow it as if your life depended on it! It does!"

The housemother inspects my luggage.

"Looks like you've brought everything you own! You'd better start unpacking!"

She walks over to the chest of drawers and pulls open the top drawer and paws through the contents. I can't believe what I'm seeing. How dare she! What is she looking for?

"This drawer is your roommate's." She pulls out a lower drawer that's empty. "Here, you can use this one!"

The housemother starts for the door, stops, turns back. "Your roommate should be here any minute. She's a Senior. We weren't able to arrange a room for you with the rest of your class on the second floor."

"Oh, great!" I groan to myself, "just great! Just my typical luck! With such a good start, what's next?"

"Set your alarm for 5:00 a.m. if you want to take a shower! Everybody — that includes you — must have breakfast and be on duty at 7:00 a.m. sharp! No lingering allowed here, Grey! You got lots to learn!"

Didn't I know it! I try to smile. "It was nice to meet you."

The housemother gives me a look that tells me 'You have not a clue as to what you're in for' but says outloud, "Dinner this afternoon in the cafeteria starts at five!"

The housemother marches off leaving the door open.

I want to ask, "Where's the cafeteria?" but I think better of it. I wasn't hungry anyway.

I sink down onto my bed. I have been here less than an hour and I am already exhausted. I feel as if I have been bullied; I feel isolated and (I hate to admit) homesick. I wish Aunt Jessie were here, but she isn't. Now as I imagine that brown Chevy moving away and disappearing, she seems so far away she might as well be on another world.

I finally get up and start to unpack. I pull out photos of my mother, my dad, my grandmother, Aunt Jessie. I consider putting them in the drawer. I consider what I have lived through this far, note again how everyone here is addressed by last name, and I begin to wonder if the same practice is followed in other schools of nursing, especially those connected to a college or university. All that has happened so far at County seems rather rough and tough like I imagine the military.

L.A. High was not like this nor was UCLA and especially not the Hollywood Professional School and I decide not to mention to anyone that I have gone to both. I know the likely response: "What are you doing here?" I consider who would most likely ask that question. I find out soon enough.

When two young women enter the room, both have two black stripes on their caps signifying they have survived to become Seniors. Neither of them seem very friendly. I can tell from her manner and her expression that my roommate is just as upset about having a Probie as a roommate as I am having to room with a Senior. Following a brief introduction, my roommate with her friend whom I learn is her rotation partner on the wards sit on my roommate's bed. Neither one appears very attractive, and for being Seniors, they just look very ordinary young women.

When she sees me put my father's portrait photo into a drawer, my roommate asks, "Who's that? He's good looking! Why are you putting him there? You mad at him?"

"Not anymore." I answer quietly. "He's my dad. I just haven't seen him in a long time."

But inside, I know how angry I really am at him for just disappearing from my life and deserting me, and because of him, here I am in this strange, forbidding place confronted by these two obnoxious Seniors.

They both smile, but I get the feeling that they are about to give me a bad time, something easy enough to do since I feel very nervous and alone and anxious about being a newcomer in what appears a hostile environment. I had certainly expected things to be different; I had at least expected to be with my classmates who were probably as apprehensive. I hadn't expected to have a housemother who was a former guard at the women's state prison. And now these two obnoxious Seniors? But Aunt Jessie would say: "That's life – get used to it!"

The two Seniors arrange themselves on the bed across from me as if they were about to assume the role of judges, a superior smirk on their faces. Here it comes. They are going to try to scare me. That shouldn't be too difficult.

I tell my roommate about the housemother going through her clothing. Both almost at the same time tell me that what I had seen was no surprise to them. They tell me that the old guard always searches their bags for drugs every time they leave the residence and when they enter. I am shocked at anyone even suspected of trying to smuggle drugs out of the hospital and even more shocked that everyone's bags would be routinely searched as if smuggling drugs in or out was routine.

My roommate informs me students sometimes use a dealer who sells them Benzedrine tables everyone calls "bennies from heaven," and students also take Ritalin tablets from the shelves of ward medical supply rooms because these medications help with the fatigue everyone feels from working so hard. Of course, both Seniors insist that they never take any drugs!

Then, as if they have done so before, they take turns describing work on the wards that is so exhausting and gross and how glad they will be to get out of County. They look at my schedule and tell me that 9A – Women's Medical Ward where I eventually will be working is a hell hole if there ever was one. They tell me they are sorry for me and list every reason why I should quit right now and spare me a tour of the wards and especially spare me my first day on duty which will be even worse. They tell me of bedsores and maggots and old ladies with ribbons in their greasy, gray, thinning hair. They ramble on about dementia and patients who scream in pain and old women who just scream. By the time they finish, I feel like not just leaving, but running – no – galloping away from this place.

By now the Seniors are laughing at my obvious open-mouthed response.

"It's not so bad, Grey! You'll get used to it by the time you get your Senior stripes! Look at us! Look how happy we are to get a chance to help people! Isn't that why we enrolled in County? Help people! What a joke! You don't have time to talk with patients let alone take care of them!

So what's on your agenda for tomorrow? Oh boy! You get to meet the faculty – lucky you! That should be enlightening! Then you get a tour of the hospital. They'll tell you how big it is – right!—as if you're so dumb you haven't noticed! Then they will take you on a tour of a ward, most likely the most gross. You'll get to meet the head nurse and view the patients. Not pretty, not pretty at all. You'll wonder, "What am I doing here!" If you're smart, you'll run! Forget your pride! Forget your luggage! Just run like you were escaping from Hell!"

While I stare at them in disbelief, my roommate studies my list of appointments. "Well, let's see what else you have coming up. Oh no! You're on the list to see Miss Loftus."

"Who's Miss Loftus?"

"The school counselor — a very scary woman."

"Why is she so scary?"

"You'll find out soon enough!"

I study them studying me studying them waiting for them to laugh uproariously at my obvious response. Instead, both inform me that they are hungry but won't eat much of whatever is offered at the cafeteria, they informing me not to expect a gourmet meal since the quality of food would gag a maggot. But I'm not that hungry anyway and I'm not sure I can locate the cafeteria. I had wanted to ask the housemother but her attitude made me decide not to try, and I'm sure I don't want to ask the two Seniors who finally leave and I find Dad's mutilated picture in my suitcase.

I suddenly feel such anger at Babu and my dad, I take the mutilated photo out of the frame, tear it up into what must be a hundred pieces, and toss them in a wastebasket. Then I cautiously follow the two Seniors at a respectful distance as they stride with knowing confidence across to the towering hospital.

Late afternoon, mostly by accident following the colored lines on the tiled floor directing me to various parts of the hospital, I find the corridor leading to the cafeteria. I recognize some whom I had seen earlier in the foyer of our student housing. One of them who appears older than the rest rises from a table where several are seated, comes to introduce herself as Jan McKinney, and invites me to join them at their table. I thank her and sit in the space they open for me.

Jan seems confident and in complete control and helps us begin to know each other: So where are you from? What high school did you go to? Why did you decide to come to L.A. County? Some had heard County was a tough school but that they would learn a lot. And each of us in turn reveal something of ourselves.

The Seniors were right. No gourmet meals here. Our first meal chicken fricassee looks like vomit, doesn't taste much better, and would, indeed, most likely gag a maggot. After this meal of which I eat little, I ask Zan and Linda if they'd like to stop by my room, and they eagerly agree.

To my relief, my roommate isn't there, so we can talk openly about our former lives and why we decided to train in nursing. Zan who is pretty and pleasant in appearance with blue eyes, brown hair in pageboy fashion tells us what sounds like a normal childhood growing up in Salem, Oregon without having any big adolescent traumas to report and that she came into nursing to have a profession that would help people. Linda who seems always ready to have fun even though she sometimes sounds cynical about life looks like a naughty elf with green eyes, red hair in a short ponytail and bangs. She, too, like me, speaks bitterly about her father and family. Bored to death in Des Moines, Iowa, she hated the place. Linda soon reveals herself openly as quite rebellious, Linda's favorite line, "The only way you can get along in this life is to take a 'I don't give a damn attitude!' about anything that happens or anything you do."

I just tell them that my dad is a writer of screenplays, and when they ask if he has written any of the recent popular movies, I reveal that he wrote the screenplay for *City Beneath the Sea*, and they seem impressed. I talk a little about Mother, a star in silent movies and a few early talking films who like all her friends had died of TB. Zan and Linda tell me how sorry they are hearing of my loss.

I talk about going home on Friday for the weekend and how I dread dealing with Babu, so I tell them a little about her and her mercurial moods. Then I explain that I'm going back to Babu's house because I do need to work and earn money to pay for books and uniforms and fees since Babu is not offering me any financial support. So I talk about my weekend job as an elevator operator at the May Company Wilshire, something I won't be able to do once I finish classes and start work on the hospital wards.

When my roommate returns, I introduce my new friends. She's polite, but you can tell that she's annoyed by having her space violated by Probies. Linda and Zan note her attitude and rise to leave. "Got to get ready for the big day tomorrow!" My roommate with a knowing smile watches them go out the door.

With the room cleared of Probies, she settles to read and I keep unpacking my favorite books and magazines.

She pauses in her reading, "You won't have time to read all that stuff here!" she warns and returns to her magazine. At 10:00 p.m., she says: "I'm going to sleep. Five o'clock comes pretty quick."

We undress, pull back our covers. On getting into bed, I find my sheets labeled L.A. County Morgue. By then I have insomnia. I'm not used to having a roommate, I don't like her, and she snores. If I were alone I would turn on my radio, listen to blues or spirituals, something I did almost every night at Babu's, carried away by the music and the lyrics, feeling myself beginning to relax, slowly sinking to sleep. Instead, I set my alarm for 4:30 hoping I won't wake my roommate. I've been getting up at 4:30 for years to study. I love the very early morning when I have the world to myself and I can get a jumpstart on the day. I'll be able to shower before she even wakes up, and I might even have time to read something for fun or encouragement. I hope training gets better! This first day has been pure misery! I recall what Dad always warned: "Be careful what you wish for!" But had I ever really wished for this?

The next morning, I wake before the alarm, something I will continue doing throughout my three years of training until I experience burnout in my Senior year. I go to find the public showers but after quickly using one, I soon will avoid them and resort to sponge baths. Returning to my room to dress, but too anxious to read, especially with my roommate busily preparing for the day, I leave and follow other Probies, catching up with Zan and Linda as we cross to the hospital and up the massive stairs beneath the statues of Hippocrates, Galen, Harvey, Pasteur.

Students are noisy this morning. Everyone seems anxious. Our new life begins. After an early breakfast of what appears to be burnt toast and watery gruel, most likely to show us what patients have to endure, we meet the full faculty of instructors and several nursing administrators. We file into a large auditorium and sit on metal chairs and study a row of women who appear old sitting on stage in starched uniforms facing us. They have highly individual caps representing the various schools of nursing where they had trained. A woman with graying hair, wire-rimed spectacles, and spotless, crisp uniform approaches the podium, Mildred Brown, Director, a graduate of Los Angeles County Hospital School of Nursing. [9]

She welcomes us warmly and gives a reverent speech about the importance of Capping, "a special event in the life of a nursing student, a solemn rite of attainment and achievement on having completed the probationary period." Receiving our caps at the end of our first months as probationers will signify that we have proven ourselves capable of progressing toward becoming a nurse, "a step up the ladder toward the ultimate goal of receiving the black velvet band to be placed across the brim of the cap. Though a nurse's cap cost little, the right to wear it could not be bought with money but must be earned by meeting professional standards. Family and friends will be invited to participate in the celebration." [10]

She ends by offering a version of looking to the right, looking to the left wondering which one of us won't get our cap. Yet she appears a kindly person, and I think of how she had begun her career as I was beginning mine. I see where she has arrived after what she has accomplished through hard work, and I am a bit encouraged. Perhaps I might do the same and accomplish what she has.

Director Brown next introduces the faculty, some appearing dour and stern, some appearing pleasant and welcoming. Then she introduces Miss Loftus who doesn't look that mean. She even looks cheerful, but then lots of people appear normal and nice but are still ogres in how they act toward others. Hadn't I lived my entire life with Babu? Miss Loftus (no one would ever dare address her by her given name) has blue, piercing eyes, mouse brown hair drawn back into a bun, a slender frame, pale skin almost transparent revealed by her light, sleeveless dress on a typically hot Los Angeles day, her apparel such a contrast to the stiff uniforms of the nursing faculty.

Director Brown tells us that for the first three weeks we will attend classes and nursing arts labs and then we'll start to learn clinical practices on the medical and surgical wards and that after Capping we will rotate to all of the other various hospital specialty services: OR, Psych Ward, Violent Men Ward, Violent Women Ward, OB/GYN.

Director Brown informs us that our rotating partners with whom we will work the hospital wards are listed on the bulletin boards in our dorms. Director Brown finishes by wishing us well during training then dismisses us to tour the hospital and a med-surg ward, and I think of my roommate and her friend warning me of what to expect.

During our tour of the hospital, we are informed that the Acute Unit opened in 1934 has 60 operations performed daily in 23 operating rooms, 14 with amphitheater seating, 5 different anesthetic gases piped to each operating room and carefully guarded so that accidents are unlikely; 87 resident doctors, not including interns, 559 visiting doctors, and 1500 nurses on rotating duty. Yet afternoon visiting hours have been shortened because of insufficient nursing help that we soon learn is a persistent problem. In case of emergency or epidemic, the entire 17th floor can be used as a separate unit isolated from the rest of the hospital. The auditorium where we had met Director Brown and the faculty near the nursing school can be used by all hospital groups. A branch of the Los Angeles County Library System provides patients with books. The entire hospitals grounds located on 56 acres has 122 buildings including a psychiatric unit, communicable disease unit, tuberculosis unit, a post office, a detached leper ward, and two jails, one for men, one for women located on the 13th floor (lucky for them!). [11]

Across from the hospital, apartments for resident nurses labeled perhaps in an attempt at lame humor "Menopause Manor," resident "cottages" that actually are barracks for student nurses labeled "Virgin Villa," and barracks for most recent interns labeled "Shangri-La". Those barracks would be torn down in 1962 when a 9-story nurses residence with 375 rooms will be built, followed in 1965 by a 10-story, air-conditioned resident-intern dormitory building with olympic-sized outdoor swimming pool.

We are shown the almost half-mile tunnel leading to the original hospital that opened in the late 1800s. Side tunnels lead to the other units we have already toured, and we are told with some humor how at one time student nurses and interns held gurney races until sternly prohibited as both dangerous and undignified.

Then as a grand conclusion, crowding into elevators, rising in groups, we are shown the med-surg ward on the ninth floor where we will be working first. Despite my roommate's warning, I am shocked. All the others are horrified! What we witness is nothing like we expected! So much crowding, such chaos, so much misery all made greater by the oppressive heat, the massive hospital not having any air conditioning other than open windows with screens to keep out flies that marvelously but unsurprisingly have found their way even to this height attracted by the noisome stew, the coolest place in the hospital the morgue far below in the basement. No surprise I begin to consider: "Can I really work in such a place?" I feel fear; I feel doubt; I feel ill. Maybe Babu was right.

The head nurse explains matter-of-factly that the patient census is always very high but not normally this bad. Rooms we view are crowded with ten beds per room rather than the six as designed, so close to each other, nurses struggle to get the side rails of beds up and down. We watch an orderly trying to get a gurney to a patient in the corner of one of these crowded rooms. He has to move beds out into the corridor in order to maneuver the cart beside the patient who needs to be transported.

"Hurry up Ricardo!" the head nurse yells, "Mr. Ellis is already late getting to x-ray.!"

"I need some help, Miss Edwards!" the orderly yells. "We'll never make it!"

The tour at last ended, we are reminded that we will be in classes and labs for three weeks before we start working the wards. We feel completely overwhelmed.

During lunch in the cafeteria, we talk breathlessly about the immensity of the hospital; we talk about the grossly overcrowded ward; the old and dying patients; the noise, the rank, disgusting odors. We discuss the hurried staff and beds so jammed together that there is almost no room to let down side rails. We all express horror at what we have viewed. We never imagined we'd see anything like this, let alone having to work every day under such conditions. Maybe we should have trained at a private hospital with private rooms, fewer patients, and no crowding. This is where we will train for the next three years? Maybe we should have not enrolled in any nursing school. Maybe we chose the wrong profession. Life with Babu didn't look so bad right now.

We talk about the classes and labs we will take and how we will be glad when they're finished but dread working on the wards dealing with real patients. We discuss again our tour of the ward and how shocked we were at what we saw and how we hope we'll be able to survive to Capping. We talk about the food we were now trying to eat but we don't want to yet we had better eat it anyway because we will need the energy to survive what we will have to face.

The evening of my first full day I call my grandmother, but Babu refuses to talk to me. So I tell Aunt Jessie as calmly as I can that I'm doing all right but that this place is worse than I expected. Aunt Jessie encourages me to stay strong, but when I hang up, I feel weak and very much alone.

Tuesday through Friday of our first week we clock in and out just like employees and during the following weeks we attend classes on anatomy, physiology, pathology, pharmacology. In nursing arts lab, we are instructed on body mechanics, the use of safety restraints, and how to take temperatures both oral and rectal. In one lab, I team with Zan and Linda to perform an autopsy on a very dead cat.

One morning without an instructor present we sit in an OR amphitheater on the fifteen floor and watch an autopsy on a human cadaver, one of the many performed yearly: With Rock and Roll blaring, a black technician dressed in green scrubs, surgical cap and gloves removes organs and throws them onto a scale to be weighed. Throughout this awful ordeal, not one word of explanation is uttered. At the end of the autopsy, everyone in the theatre is silent. An intern stands, stretches and asks:

"Everybody ready for lunch?"

Filing into the cafeteria we all feel ill. We wonder if the autopsy we had just witnessed was planned to shock us and shake out the students who won't be able to cope. We comment on some students leaving the amphitheater rather than suffer through the ordeal, and we wonder if they probably might quit school. Then even more sickening than what we had witnessed, while going through the foodline, we discover that for lunch we are having some mess consisting of noodles and hamburger that seems too much like the intestines we had just witnessed being sliced and diced during autopsy.

As bad as all that, a few days later I can't believe what I am witnessing when the neurologist takes up a brain once belonging to a human, drops it on a platter, slices it, passes the platter around the class, then dumps what's on the platter into a garbage can. An intern and I exchange looks, mine of shock, his, acquired indifference.

During lunch breaks in the cafeteria, getting to know each other, we pretty much group together, Probies sit with Probies, Juniors with Juniors, Seniors with Seniors. I'm getting to know Linda and Zan (whom I learn is my partner when we rotate the various services), and we now have the basis for a close friendship. We discuss our stupid textbook with its section on housekeeping urging us to maintain a clean, orderly, peaceful environment for patients. Right! Our meal again of some semblance of a fricassee looks more like creamed, scrambled brain.

Friday afternoon and I'm packing to go home for the weekend, throwing a few things into my suitcase that has already begun to look battered. I wish I never had to go back to Babu's, but must for now. I ask Zan and Linda what they will do. Linda probably will stay at the hospital. Zan is going to stay with an aunt and uncle who reside somewhere in the L.A. area. When I leave, my bag and suitcase are searched by our former prison guard housemother. What is she looking for? My morgue sheets? Drugs! Do I look like someone who would steal drugs!

"You never can tell," she replies with a stern, steady gaze. "The most innocent-looking are the most likely."

My first bus ride home from the hospital will take three transfers and just about two hours. I should bring water but have no way to carry it, bottled water not available, soda always with sugar and caffeine only available in glass bottles. A very hot and smoggy Friday, the buses are crowded, no empty benches at transfer points, the benches occupied by old women and pregnant Latina mothers with toddlers, a long, tiring wait between buses running late because it's Friday and traffic is typical L.A.

I suddenly understand the line from *Sunset Boulevard*: "In L.A., you can get along without your morals but not your car."

I hate to think about taking this bus trip back and forth every weekend with fewer buses running on Sunday and even longer waits, but I know I will have to endure this trip for now after everything else I have to survive at County. Finally reaching my old neighborhood, I descend from the third bus at Crenshaw and Wilshire. There on one side of the street is a big mansion with seven chimneys and shuttered windows where *Sunset Boulevard* was once filmed and sometimes my friend Paula and I used to trespass and play there. [Paula Strahm, Ramona's life-long friend, suggests in an email that she and another friend had played in the mansion. "I don't recall ever going to the mansion with Ramona to play. Her mother and grandmother were far too protective of her to let her do that."]

Traffic is so heavy, I have to wait to cross the street and then walk the long way from Wilshire to the beautiful Dutch Colonial house with its rose arbor above the walkway to the door. When I enter and call out a greeting, despite seeing the furnishings, the carpeting, the drapery, everything I have lived with for years, I suddenly feel I am no longer at home.

My first night back at Babu's, the situation starts out OK, but then goes south during dinner. Babu always cooks a great leg of lamb or stew and always has the same meals in order each day of the week since for a while we had a boarding house. Every Christmas we had a hugh feast with preparations starting at five o'clock in the morning, Babu supervising the entire meal then suddenly becoming very ill when dinner is over and everyone else required to clean up after. She would have to be helped to her bed while the rest of us cleared the table and did the dishes. Her sudden after dinner collapse from fatigue got to be an annual event as regular as Christmas and a bit of a joke.

Johnnie and Aunt Jessie want to know every detail about my first week at County. How many patients have I cared for? I explain that we won't have patients for the first three weeks while in classes and labs, not until we start on the wards. Babu looks discussed.

"No patients yet! What kind of training are you getting! When I was in training, I was on duty the very first day! We scrubbed floors, bed pans, utility rooms! We had no book learning. Just hard work! Lots of it scrubbing floors, cleaning bedpans. After the first week we bathed patients, fed them, made beds. After three weeks we began to have time for study but only after the day's work on the wards was done. I thought you would be exhausted and ready to quit!"

She seems disappointed that I don't appear half dead although I feel like it.

"But that time will come, young lady – believe me! They're babying you right now, but that will end, believe me, that will end! Things will get hard, and you'll want to come home. You'll find out nursing is hard, dirty work!"

I feel myself getting angry. Babu has the gift of saying the wrong words just to me, never to anyone else. Aunt Jessie tries to defuse the situation by asking me if I had begun making friends.

But before I can answer telling them about Zan and Linda, Babu starts in again.

"I've always said better to aim high and miss than aim low and hit what's easy! Why nursing? You know you could be a doctor! You could be something I'd be proud of and not just a glorified maid!"

Babu was saying almost exactly the same words she'd been saying over and over for months. She hated the fact I was going into nursing because it allowed me to get away from her.

"I was always so proud of your mother. She used her talent. She was already a star when she met your father, got sick, and died. It makes my blood boil just to think about it!"

Babu always claimed her greatest achievement was promoting my mother to become a film star who acted in thirty-three silent films during the 1920's, and five Spanish-language films made during the 1940's in Argentina where she met my father [12]. Babu's church and her nursing and physical therapy practices were also her achievements, and Babu was well-known known as a healer, almost a worker of miracles, and many thought her as a wonderful friend to have.

Well, she wasn't my friend! I wanted to tell her where to go! But what was the use? She would only yell at me for using such language: "Was that what they teach you at County?"

Instead, I get up, take up my dishes and start for the kitchen.

"I didn't excuse you, young lady! Just because you moved out of this house doesn't mean you can disrespect me!"

Babu dislikes laxness and failure to meet obligations, another reason she especially dislikes my father who never paid a cent for my support or for my mother's care. She always disliked my arriving home late even five minutes without informing her of why I might be late. She hated people who lied. But above all, she mostly disliked people who showed her disrespect.

Aunt Jessie says nothing and just continues eating. I know she wants to get up and follow me to the kitchen, but another all out war would break loose if she did since she would appear to be supporting me.

She glances at me. Her eyes and expression tell me, ("Be quiet, Mona. I don't feel up to this tonight.")

"I'm sorry Babu," I offer. "I am really tired and I have to get ready for work tomorrow." I sigh thinking to myself, "Another long day lay ahead, another long day of going up and down, up and down."

When you are in an elevator operator at the May Company Wilshire wearing heels and a navy blue dress like a uniform, the first hour isn't too bad. You get to say "hello" to customers who appear interesting and chat with people who work at the May Company Wilshire, staff members I meet in the lunchroom who are pleasant and friendly even though most are screenwriters without producers, actors without film roles, musicians without orchestras, all hoping to be noticed and heard by somebody or anybody. But after the first hour, going up and down starts to get tiring, even though we do have some interesting customers, some obviously of wealth wearing fashionable clothes and lots of jewelry with real gemstones (no costume jewelry for these ladies) their hair lightened or dyed every week without a strand out of place. Many of our customers are wealthy, the May Company attracting customers from Beverly Hills and Bel Air which aren't that distant. We even sometimes see movie stars: One time I took Za Za Gabor to the 5th floor offering exclusive designer clothes for women. But too many customers seem snobbish, either ignoring me completely or looking at me with complete disdain, as if I weren't glamorous enough to interest them. They make me feel like a servant, just as Babu claims.

During my long day at May Company Wilshire, I think often about patients on the Women's Ward at County: old, sick, dying, dressed in stained hospital gowns, bright ribbons in their greasy hair. One bit of relief during my day, I have an acquaintance who is also an elevator operator and she and I ride up and down with each other during our breaks just for company to keep the boredom from killing us. By the end of the day, I feel exhausted from taking too many haughty snobs up and down for eight hours so they can shop and mistreat the sales staff as if they were servants.

Oh, well, this job is the only way I am going to get any money. Babu won't give me any, Aunt Jessie doesn't have any, and I don't know where my father is, most likely celebrating the success of his movie *City Beneath the Sea*, not that he'd help me anyway. He's too cheap! Finally at quitting time preparing myself for whom I know all to well and what is waiting, I get on a bus and go back to Babu's.

Returning to County on Sunday night after a weekend with Babu seems good to be getting back and seeing my new friends Zan and Linda. I tell them about my miserable time at Babu's and the boring time at the May Company. Linda, as I had guessed, just stayed at the hospital, and she already had met some guy who delivers supplies to all the hospital units. Meeting guys apparently is one of Linda's sports, and she doesn't give a damn who they are as long as they give her the good time she wants. Zan doesn't say much about her weekend. I never really do learn much about the aunt and uncle she says she stays with on weekends. I go to my room where, of course, I find my dear roommate and her good buddy. I don't feel like dealing with them right now or ever. I know they want to grill me about my weekend, but I brush them off by telling them it was tiring and boring. They then start to ask me about my schedule for the new week. I tell them the most exciting thing I am going to do is continue my autopsy of a cat. And I have an appointment with Miss Loftus on Thursday. Both Seniors grimace.

"Oh, oh! That's bad. Real bad. Have any other Probies seen Miss Loftus yet?

"No, Not that I'm aware of. Why?" As always, I can feel my ever-present anxiety begin to stir.

"Well, if you're one of the first Probies, even if not the first she sees, (the word "probie" always uttered with a certain amount of condescension) I'd say you have a problem."

"Problem? Why is that?" My anxiety goes up another notch!

"Well, Miss Loftus always sees first those Probies she's worried about.

"Why would she be worried about me? I'm fine."

"Well, apparently she must not think you're fine. She's a psychologist – a Freudian psychologist. Do you know who Freud is?"

"Of course I know who Freud is! I took a psychology class at UCLA! Freud is all about the subconscious mind and defense mechanisms."

"Well, all we can say is good luck with concealing your defense mechanisms. Loftus will try to delve into your subconscious. If you let her dig deep enough and she finds something she doesn't like, you're history. You won't last long at County."

"And for heaven's sake, you'd better tell her you have a boyfriend!"

"Boyfriend! Why should I tell her I have a boy friend!"

"You'll find out, Probie. We've got to go. Catch you later."

And they were gone, leaving me alone with my growing anxiety.

Wednesday, the night before I see Miss Loftus, I've worried about our meeting since Sunday when I talked with the two Seniors and they warned me what to expect. I'm aware that I have an unusual background growing up in Hollywood, my mother a successful movie star, my dad a playwright and screenplay writer. I went to the

Hollywood Professional School, a very different kind of school in order to be able to go out on auditions for roles in film. Normal kids don't do that. They join clubs, play sports, expect they'll get married and have 2.5 kids some day. I changed my name after my mother suddenly died. Why?

All these facts would be of great, even morbid interest to a Freudian psychologist like Miss Loftus who had the power to get me kicked out of training if she decided I had too many problems preventing me from becoming a nurse. I began to imagine what I would face if I had to go back to Babu and her sneering condemnation about my failure, and that possibility, of course, only increases my anxiety. I try talking to Zan and Linda about my worry regarding my background, but we have known each other such a short time they really don't know how I feel. With no one I really can talk to, as always, I talk to myself, but I never offer myself much comfort.

I don't sleep Wednesday night imagining all kinds of scenarios, all of them bad. My anxiety building all week now is reaching climax. Finally I decide that Miss Loftus couldn't be much worse to deal with then Babu, and at least I didn't have to live with Loftus. The problem is that Miss Loftus has power, knows she has power, and uses it. I'm afraid she will use it on me.

Thursday, the day I have to meet Loftus has been a rotten day: I'm exhausted from no sleep, hardly able to complete my school assignments, distracted by worry from following the lectures in class. I feel even more anxious as I wait in the corridor outside Miss Loftus' office where I hear her talking with another student, some poor girl whom I can't understand because she is speaking so softly, probably beaten down by her inquisitor. I have nothing to look at and distract my attention except for a hugh photo of Los Angles County General Hospital in all of its massive, overwhelming glory. [13]

And as I stare at the huge photo, the hospital appears to grow bigger and bigger and bigger until it looks to my mind disoriented by lack of sleep as if it is preparing to burst out of its frame and swallow me, the hallway itself crashing over me, crushing me beneath a gigantic pile of granite, black marble, and concrete.

A young woman I recognize suddenly emerges from the office in tears. She glances at me and hurries past me down the hall and is gone.

"Miss Grey!"

I get up slowly and move toward the yawning door of her chamber of horrors.

"Come in, Miss Grey. I'm Amy Loftus, your counselor. Have a seat."

Miss Loftus and I don't sit at her desk. Instead we sit in two chairs that place us directly across from each other allowing her to observe my every expression, my every move, or anything I did that might signal anxiety or anger or fear, observations that in my present obvious condition are not at all difficult. Miss Loftus starts examining my file. Watching Miss Loftus makes me more anxious, but waiting also gives me the opportunity to observe my supposed counselor, a plain looking, thirty-something woman in sensible shoes, light, brown hair pulled back in a bun so currently popular, and a light, sleeveless dress on another hot day in Los Angeles.

Miss Loftus continues searching through my file. Finally, after studying one page for what seems too long, Miss Loftus looks at me and smiles grimly.

"Well, Miss Grey, it appears we have a number of problems to work on."

Alarm bells go off in my brain. "Problems?"

Miss Loftus seems impatient. "Yes, problems!"

My apprehension grows. "Problems? Are they serious?"

Miss Loftus looks at me as if I am extremely dense and surely a budding psychotic.

"Serious enough. In fact, we almost didn't admit you to our school because of potential problems."

I can't believe what I am hearing! My mind starts scanning the major events that have occurred during my eighteen years, and I can't readily recall anything I had done that would warrant my not being admitted to Los Angeles County General Hospital School of Nursing. I reach my hand toward Miss Loftus.

"May I please look at my file?"

Miss Loftus closes the file and places it on her desk out of my reach. "Your file is confidential, Miss Grey!

A bolt of anger passes through me, heating my brain. I feel a compulsion to scream, "That's my file! I have a right to know what's in it and what you're basing your accusations on and why you decided that I should not have been admitted to this school!"

I feel a compulsive desire to get up, grab my file, run out of the office, go to my room, and read every word of it, no matter how painful or disturbing. But I can't do all that. I can't leave. All I can do is sit trapped in this office in sweltering heat.

I gaze at the fan in the corner of the room and pray Miss Loftus will turn it on. How can she abide such heat in this room with no open windows, a room that seems closing in on me? Perhaps a woman as cold as she could never really get warm. As I study Miss Loftus, I can tell she knows how disturbed I am. I'm sure she can see the mix of confusion and resentment in my eyes.

Cool and composed despite the stifling heat, she takes my file back off her desk and picks up her pen. We study each other in the silence and heavy heat. Finally, I feel calm enough to speak quietly.

"Miss Loftus, what exactly are my problems?"

Miss Loftus begins by asking me about my name change. She asks me to discuss my family history, and I confess that, yes, I am angry because of my mother suddenly dying, my father disappearing, my grandmother always resenting having to raise me because I was more like my father in name and appearance and not more like my mother. I tell her I decided to change my name and be reborn after my mother died and my father abandoned me. From a story my mother told me about a man who left his wife to get a pack of cigarettes and then never came back, I always feared being abandoned. I always knew that I would have to face my mother's death at some time but she seemed so well until it happened.

I recall all too clearly the night my mother died: Mother had seemed she was doing well, but she kept clearing her throat. I knew that Babu was afraid and so was my dad because tuberculosis doesn't just affect the lungs. It also ravages the bones and the larynx. Bacteria have a field day destroying the tissues of someone already weakened and exhausted from the ravages of pulmonary infection. No surprise that tuberculosis, "The White Plague," is called consumption. Babu and Dad knew that tuberculosis was slowly but surely consuming my mother who also knew a severe problem developing in her larynx caused her to constantly clear her throat.

At that time, three drugs had just been developed and approved. But my mother who, thanks to one of my make-believe aunts, had completely converted to Christian Science and refused to take them, my mother insisting she was doubtful of medical procedures that caused her weariness and pain but didn't help cure her disease. In addition, despite the effects of tuberculosis, Mother was still as beautiful as ever although it was destroying her lungs and larynx and she was dying in the same way as so many of Mother's friends she had met at a sanitarium for treating tuberculosis where they all had waited hoping for a cure, yet when it came, while others eagerly accepted, Mother had refused.

Yet no matter what Mary Baker Eddy said in her revered book on which Christian Science was founded, mother was dying. Yet, she believed! Yes, she truly believed since she had seen my play-aunt healed, the people who spoke at the testimonials every Wednesday night were healed. Why shouldn't Mother be healed? She could call her Christian Science counselor anytime day or night to confirm her fanatical belief that Christian Science would bring back her health since it taught that illness was an illusion, that God was good, and that God never created illness that was evil, therefore illness did not exist. So because of the teaching of Christian Science, my make-believe aunt's seeming complete recovery from a less deadly disease, the Wednesday night testimonials of the true believers grateful for their recovery from some mild or common illness, and the support of her counselor night and day, Mother believed absolutely that she, too, would be healed from this illusion that had not been created by God who is loving, all-knowing, benevolent. Having become a true believer, Mother absolutely refused to even consider taking the new drugs that were curing tuberculosis patients and saving them from an early grave.

My grandmother tried to talk some sense into her daughter's head so filled with foolish desperate dreams of recovery. My father, under some ill-conceived notion that he could persuade her to give up her fanatical belief threatened to divorce Mother if she didn't take the new medicines. I begged my mother again and again to please take the medications, please get well, please not die, please, please don't leave me alone in a harsh world controlled and dominated by Babu.

Mother said, "NO!" Her Christian Science said, NO!" My play-aunt said, NO!" Mary Baker Edie had said "NO!" in her book that claimed any supposed illness such as tuberculosis did not exist and is just an illusion, a nightmare from which the faithful true believers would awaken, while all wretched unbelievers were condemned to watch the most important persons in their lives die from a disease that was actually a terrible disease consuming its victims that could be destroyed once effective drugs were available.

So the disease that was supposedly only an illusion drained all my mother's strength and she died. And I still clearly recall the whole terrible incident burned forever into my soul.

The night Mother died she was well enough to take me to our usual Friday night movie at the theatre on Wilshire and Western that was screening *Brute Force* starring Burt Lancaster as a convict trying to escape prison. Burt Lancaster was my favorite actor in a role emerging in films at that time of a powerful anti-hero who wasn't all bad, and we often went to see such films more than once. That night after we returned from the movie seemed like any ordinary night. Mother came in my room after I was in bed, my radio turned on low to my favorite program of spirituals. Babu, of course, didn't like my choice of music but Mother did.

Mother kissed me and said "Good night, darling. Sleep well. I'll see you in the morning."

I watched her walk out of the dark room into the light and then was gone.

I fell asleep with the radio left playing softly, the songs continuing to play through the night. I woke up several times and listened to the sad lyrics, the singer pleading for freedom from sorrow and pain, a better life for her children, pleading for forgiveness, for salvation, for courage at the hour of death.

I suddenly woke to hear Babu screaming. Her loud, desperate screams could mean only one thing. Mother was dead! I thought 'Oh no! Please, God, no!' But this was no dream, no nightmare from which I would eventually wake!

Aunt Jessie opened my door. She looked shocked. Even though Aunt Jessie knew this blow, this assault on my mother and the rest of us was coming and indeed inevitable, she didn't expect it quite so soon. Yet it had been only a matter of time and the time was now.

I went to Mother's bedroom door and saw her lying face down on the floor in a pool of blood. Babu kept screaming over and over,

"Oh my baby! Oh my baby!"

I felt afraid, frozen. I stood in the doorway and watched Babu scream while mother lay silent on the floor.

What I was witnessing was true and immediate and real. My mother was gone. She had left me alone with Babu.

Mother apparently had gotten up to get help because she was starting to hemorrhage from her mouth, but instead she fell to the floor and died.

After the coroner came to pick up my mother, Babu stopped screaming and called Mother's Christian Science counselor who did admit that, yes, of course, my mother had called him, that she had told him she was bleeding from the mouth more than a trickle, the bleeding a sudden gush. Mother's counselor had calmly told Mother to keep her faith and remember that all of what was happening was only an illusion and that through her faith she would be all right.

My grandmother asked "Why didn't you call me? Maybe I could have helped her! Maybe I could have saved her!"

Mother's counselor said that he felt that my mother's faith was so strong it would save her and that she would be all right. He told Babu that he wasn't worried about Mother's condition. He knew how strongly Mother believed. Then he hung up."

After Mother's death, I, always very serious about life, wrote a play in which everyone died leaving me quite alone. My mother's death the worst event that ever happened to me, I would cry myself to sleep for a number of years recalling Mother's death, and I conclude that the death of a parent you love is a wound that never heals.

I often thought of Mother's beautiful friends, especially one only 24 years old, and I remember standing before the screened window of the young woman's bedroom, not allowed in to visit because the young woman was dying of tuberculosis. I also recall another friend of Mother's, a beautiful girl who died young, the girl's mother saying to Babu: "Why did my daughter die and not yours!" Well, my mother, Babu's daughter, died soon after, and I've often wondered whether the woman was somehow helped and satisfied by Mother's death.

After my mother died and until I graduated from high school I became religious and virtuous to an absurd degree. I explored many religions, Catholic, Hebrew, Mormon, Hindu, but I finally took an extreme interest in Catholicism and even wanted to become a nun, even though I wasn't a Catholic, had never been confirmed in the faith, had never been to mass or confession or communion. The idea of being a nun seemed safe and secure and all that devotion and my consuming interest in the lives of the saints especially Joan of Arc whose given name I took as my own that saved me from bizarre behavior or suicide. However crazy I must have seemed to others, through my faith I didn't feel alone, and I believed that I would eventually go to heaven and be with my mother whom I missed terribly, especially with my grandmother dominating my every move and almost my every thought.

[Paula Strahm in an email reports that after Ramona's mother died, Ramona told Paula she was so depressed she ran away from her grandmother's home, arrived at a nearby convent, and told them she wanted to be a nun.]

Another source of refuge, I always had my nose in a book. I loved books of all kinds. Mother would take me to the library on Saturdays when she was well enough while on medications she ultimately refused, and I would go home with a stack of books about the Greek and Roman gods until I ran out of books on those gods and started on the Viking gods, although I didn't like them nearly as well. I also read biographies about nurses, both famous nurses and student nurses and also famous women who were actresses or doctors or scientists, and I had a set of books of famous people I loved to read over and over.

Miss Loftus in response to what I tell her informs me that she had voted against my being admitted to the school of nursing because she thinks that children who lose a parent, especially a mother, never fully recover from the loss. Such an abiding sense of loss felt as rejection she believes will severely affect my ability to care for patients. Miss Loftus sighs almost in resignation.

"So, Miss Romero, or Grey, as you now prefer, your major problem is your family background and the way you were parented. Although we decided on the basis of your transcripts that you would do well academically, we thought that you might not have the special qualities required to become a good nurse."

I feel insulted as if she had slapped my face.

Ignoring my obvious shock, she continues, "Some students come into nursing because they want to get away from home. Have you ever wanted to leave home?"

I hesitate. I know I need to be careful how I answer her. "Sometimes I have," I admit weakly.

"Why!"

"My grandmother took care of me after my mother died. We didn't always get along." I also want to add, "*because Babu was as mean as you!*" but I remain mute.

"How about your father? Where is he?"

"I have no idea. I haven't seen him in years. He disappeared after mother died. He and my grandmother didn't get along either."

"Miss Grey, my questions concerning your problems are not about anything you have done yet, at least not here in our school. My concerns are about some disturbing indications on your psychological tests that most likely stem from your background and the way you were nurtured in an environment void of parents."

Problems? What problems? Tests? What tests? Those I took for being admitted to the school of nursing? My transcripts from high school or UCLA or Hollywood Professional School?

"I understand that you were involved in acting and had even auditioned apparently without success for at least two films that became very popular and are now considered classics. Is that why you gave up your ambition of becoming an actress and film star?"

What was I suppose to answer? What could I say? Should I admit that someone with more talent and experience than I had won the part because she had acted in other films, and I had been just a bit player in some community theater productions of plays mostly written by my father?

"In addition, Miss Grey, your application papers for admission including statements of recommendations from those with whom you studied indicate that you had studied piano for several years and were accomplished and that you had performed at invitational recitals, one at the Hollywood Bowl. Why did you abandon that promising career path? Instead, you want to become a nurse? Do you fully understand what your duties as a nurse will involve?"

She studies me and waits for me to answer, but how can I respond when I've just started training.

"Well, Miss Grey, Let me help make clear what you have chosen to undertake. First, I want to describe for you L.A. County General Hospital and what training here requires. As you have learned in the last week or so, this hospital is one of the largest in the world. We have a yearly bed count that ranges between 3,000 and 6,000 very sick patients and often dying patients. In fact, as we sit here in this office, there are patients all over this hospital who are dying. Some are lucky enough to have a relative or friend at their side, but many die alone."

Miss Loftus stops and takes a deep breath. My counselor suddenly appears as a mediocre actress speaking her lines while studying me for my reaction, auditioning for a dramatic role she will never win.

"Now let us imagine that you have been assigned to a men's medical ward. Today, as is typical, there is a bed count of seventy patients, and the ward, as usual, is very short staffed. Even though you're a student, you're expected to shoulder heavy responsibilities that shouldn't be yours until you graduate. Right now, you are taking care of a Mr. Jones who is dying of heart failure, and he is dying without a soul with him who cares. He looks at you through eyes that are about to close forever. You grasp his hand in yours, and you tell him that you are with him, and you will not let him die alone."

Miss Loftus waits to let this point sink in.

"The only trouble with your good intentions, Miss Grey, is that Mr. Jones is one patient, and you have sixty-nine other patients who need your help! You have patients who are in pain, patients who are wondering why you haven't come with their shots or their pills, patients who need water, who need a urinal, who must be turned or their skin will break down and develop ulcers, patients who are so sick that they need constant care that you don't have the time to give them! So you slowly pull your hand away from Mr. Jones telling him you'll be back."

As she continues, I see that Miss Loftus has forgotten her clinical role as counselor and has somehow changed character, her eyes gazing past me to some place that only she can see, her words coming rapidly.

"So you rush around the ward and give the pain shots and the pain pills and get the water for the thirsty and turn the patients who have lain far too long in one position, and you check on the critically ill! Exhausted, you finally go back to Mr. Jones, and you find that he is dead and he has died alone! Consider what you have done, Miss Grey! You have broken your promise to him, Miss Grey! You have betrayed a dying man!"

Miss Loftus glares at me as she finishes. I guess this is where I'm supposed to start crying. I do want to cry, but not here, never here. I want to cry because I don't want to share with this woman any memories or any feelings I have about the death of my mother and the abandonment by my father.

Miss Loftus now returns to her cool and clinical persona. She studies me with a hard look, an accusing look, a look that says you have failed a dying man in his final moments. Somehow Miss Loftus has transformed Mr. Jones from an imaginary patient into a real person, one who has died all alone, and as Miss Loftus continues talking about Mr. Jones, I think again about my mother and how she had died alone, reaching out for help that wasn't there and never came.

"How do you think you're going to feel, Miss Grey? Are you going to feel guilty? Depressed? Angry with yourself or angry at Mr. Jones for dying before you got back to him?

All I can tell you, Miss Grey, is that we typically lose one-third to one-half of the students from each class. Some students decide to leave because they can't deal with the pressure and the demands, and they fall apart. Other students we ask leave because they are not able to function under such trying conditions and they become a hazard on the wards. I hope that I'm wrong, but I feel that your problems will eventually force you out of this school, either because you choose to leave, or we ask you to. This is why I feel that you should not have been admitted in the first place. We want students whom we believe will succeed and graduate and become good nurses. I hope you'll be one of them, but I have my doubts."

Miss Loftus glares at me again as if demanding a response. What am I supposed to say? So I remain mute, waiting.

"Can you be objective, Miss Grey? It's absolutely essential for you to realize that meeting the needs of all of your patients is more important than meeting the needs of only one patient. In a perfect world, every patient would have a private nurse, but Los Angeles County General Hospital is far from a perfect world."

She sits back in her chair to allow me to respond. What should I say? What could I say? In a perfect world, we wouldn't need nurses? But I say nothing.

"Well, Miss Grey, since you have no ready response, perhaps you need time to reflect on your choice of career. But be assured that we will meet again to discuss your problems. Now you may return to your quarters and ready yourself for your nursing studies which you apparently prefer over everything else."

Thus our first encounter draws to a close and she notes that I'll be starting on the wards in a few days. She wishes me success and tells me to come to her if I have any problems I want to discuss. How likely is that, I ask myself. Then she pulls out her appointment book and sets a date for another meeting.

Rising majestically from her chair, she waits for me to rise and walks me to the door. And while because of my fierce determination not to reveal to someone like her my true emotions, I am not yet in tears, but I now know the feelings of the young woman I had seen rush in tears from Loftus' chamber of horrors.

Once out of Miss Loftus' office, I, too, feel shaken from her trying to destroy my defenses and my self-confidence. I now know I am in a battle with Loftus for my self-esteem and my future, but I am not certain who will win.

The following day, almost as if by Miss Loftus' design, we are given a tour of the psychiatric wards by the chief psychiatrist and offered a view of the Violent Men Ward, the Violent Women Ward, and the Treatment Ward where the patients were relatively calm and where I later learn to play billiards, although I am always a bit afraid that one of the patients will suddenly go berserk and hit me with a pool stick. The chief psychiatrist shows us a leather restraint.

"Some day we won't use this barbaric way to keep a violent patient safe! With new and better medications we won't have any violent patients."

Then he tells us that when we serve on the Violent Wards, we will have to use keys on entering and exiting.

Early morning of our very first day on Women's Medical Ward when we cross from our residence to the hospital, we are all excited and anxious. We have on our uniforms for the first time: Clean white dresses, white shiny shoes, white hose with straight seams, white Probie "dunce" cap in the shape of a cone with a flattened tip, hair up off our shoulders or in a short pony tail. I look around and I feel some discomfort from this scene. I have never worn a uniform even while working at the May Company Wilshire. I have never had the feeling of being exactly like everyone else, and I don't like it. What would Loftus say about that if for whatever odd reason I told her?

We go to the cafeteria where we are offered breakfast of pale toast and thin gruel, most likely the same as what we will be serving patients. We're all unusually quiet wondering how our first day on a ward will go. Some students are going to a Men's Ward, others to a surgical ward.

Women's Medical Ward is very busy and very crowded. Zan who will be my partner when we rotate various wards looks around at all the very sick patients of whom we are supposed to take care. How are we supposed to do anything for all of them? Suddenly we feel very afraid and that we can't do the job. We're so anxious we go to our instructor and we tell her how we feel. She is very pleasant and definite in assuring us that there's no reason for us to be afraid. These patients can't hurt us and we can't do anything to hurt them because she won't let us since she will be right there beside us to help. With her words we feel less anxious but not much, yet we are determined to do what we have been taught.

Today we will do our first procedure taking temperatures. I'm selected to perform the first temperature taken rectally, my patient an elderly, senile woman unable to hold a thermometer steady in her mouth.

"Why me!" I silently complain to the patron saint I have adopted along with her name.

The instructor pulls the curtains around the bed where we are all standing, everyone waiting for me to begin. I struggle to take the side rail down and another student helps me turn the patient so that her backside faces me. I pull back the sheets and I'm staring with horror at a hugh bedsore on the patient's tail bone. We had only seen bedsores in our textbooks, but here was the real thing. I think I am going to faint. All of us feeling sick to our stomachs seeing a bad *decubitus* ulcer for the first time, our instructor explains that this bedsore is the result of neglect and never should have happened. Someone hadn't turned the patient on schedule as required. Our instructor then informs us that sometimes you can see to the bone, then adds to our horror that sometimes maggots infest the bedsore, but as horrible as they are, they actually do some good by cleaning up the wound. We are told that this patient is lucky. She has only one ulcer. Some patients also have them between their knees, some on the back of their heads.

After the instructor's explanation, I'm not able to move. I feel frozen and faint at the same time. Will I faint and fall to the floor or just stay standing like a statue.

"All right, Miss Grey, let's get started!"

My instructor's command shakes me out of my trance, and somehow I perform the procedure and I clean up the patient and bandage the ulcer while trying to make her comfortable under the watchful and critical eye of the instructor. After what seemed a long time, I finally finish and we pull back the curtain. The instructor tells me I did fine, but she will talk with me later about my technique. We leave the patient's bedside and another student takes an oral temp on the patient next too mine.

Later that same day, by my continuing good fortune, I am elected to the post of Miss Professional Standards. Having already felt alienated enough rooming with a Senior and separated from my classmates, each and every morning as my classmates climb the stairs to the hospital my duty is to inspect each of them one at a time to make sure her shoes are polished, white hose seams straight, white uniform spotless, white "dunce" cap pinned correctly to well-groomed hair, trim finger nails clean. And after only a day or two of my having this loathsome task, I know I surely will be glad when we finally get our caps, I am relieved of my hideous duty, eventually getting rid of my obnoxious roommate who will have graduated, and I will have moved to the "cottages" (aka barracks) along with my classmates when we all suddenly are Juniors. Our rooms in the barracks won't be much to write home about, but for me who never writes home I will be so much happier than I have been in that dorm apartment separated from my new friends.

We all soon learn that a typical day at County as a Probie on a ward consists of receiving reports, providing morning care and serving breakfast and feeding patients who are unable to feed themselves, giving baths, guiding oral hygiene, offering backrubs, changing beds, ambulating patients, preparing them for lunch, serving or feeding them lunch, making sure patients have had bowel movements, having a quick lunch ourselves in the cafeteria closest to our ward, then hurrying to classes in the afternoon. The ward at first seems to us to be an ugly, foul, sad, pathetic place. We are continuously anxious that we will do something wrong or stupid, and sometimes I feel like a slave toting that bar, lifting that bail, only here we tote trays of food and bedpans. We lift and turn heavy patients. We struggle with the side rails of beds with barely enough room to squeeze between the beds and then break our backs rolling the beds up and down, up and down. We soon are always exhausted from all our effort.

Ward work is not only physically tiring, it is mentally exhausting. We are always under the watchful and critical eye of an instructor and the head nurse. We better not complain or show any lack of self-confidence, especially since we learn that after Capping, advanced student nurses and interns essentially run the hospital with only the help of an aide or an orderly on a ward. But ward work more than anything is emotionally draining. Most of us are still young women, and already we have seen so much suffering. By the time we are capped, we will have matured as if we had aged ten years while wondering how many poor old souls we might have put out of their misery, accidentally, of course, as we attempt to determine what we might have done that had possibly caused their death or hastened it, and we will remark with bitter humor that we have buried our mistakes. We will wonder whether other students in other schools live and learn in what must be pleasant surroundings and are taught in bright classrooms with clean air to breath while we are trapped in an all too often smelly, sickening environment.

We do our best to care for our wards. However, we too often fail because we don't know as yet how to properly care for our patients. So no matter how much on rare occasions the instructor might praise us, everyone of us goes back to our room with a sense of fatigue and guilt from not achieving our goal of successfully helping others. Will we ever learn?

But gradually as days pass, we slowly grow accommodated to the wards. The persistent odors, the persistent crowded conditions, the suffering of patients no longer affecting us as they had when we began, and we gradually learn to accept the hard, dirty work that nursing involves. Hadn't we all willingly with great expectations eagerly signed up for what we were now doing? Yet, in our idealistic, naive souls, we struggle in our ebbing belief that we still can help all our patients who so depend on what we at first try so ineptly to do for them. As a result, our being a student at County begins making the biggest difference in our own lives. Our innocence evaporating, we develop more and more an assumed, controlled hardness because we feel we have to become "tough" as we face each new brutal day. So somehow we survive, slowly becoming the new person we didn't always like but knowing we would graduate while also knowing that achieving such a distant goal would remain a constant challenge.

No surprise, however, that some Probies are not destined to survive because they can't as readily adapt to such challenging conditions. I see everyday some students looking a little grayer, a little more nauseated, more exhausted, some beginning to feel worse then their patients. But although many Probies try to hide their state of mind, what finally becomes clear is that they have decided to leave, or they are told that they will have to leave when they can't meet the demands of our school and they are just too frightened, too shocked, and no longer can pretend to be confident when they aren't. Some don't do well in classes and labs, others without competence can't care for patients, and all those, nearly a third of the class leave, as Miss Loftus predicted, perhaps with her help, carrying a sense of shame from not measuring up as nursing students or even as caring, competent humans. And Miss Loftus steeped in theory practicing her beliefs on the weakest in too many encounters succeeds in shattering their defenses. Unable to deny and accept that they are afraid, forced to face that they have problems that make them unsuitable for nursing, they are forced out feeling defeated and a failure.

One Probie, Judy—I never know her last name—isn't just miserable or unable to do the work, she suffers a complete collapse of nerves, clearly indicating that she doesn't belong in Los Angeles County General Hospital School of Nursing. Tall, thin, with short, blond, curly hair, she jumps, flinches, looking nervously over her shoulder the whole time she is on the wards. In nursing labs she tries to perform a procedure always without success, so I am not surprised when poor Judy finally cracks like an egg. How I find out about Judy is a shock.

Walking down a corridor of the hospital where there are private rooms, I hear a female voice cry out "No! No!!" I stop and look through the partially open door, and there I see Judy in cloth restraints held down on a gurney by two nurses, Judy twisting her head from side to side struggling to get free. One nurse suddenly spotting me staring at Judy from the hallway walks over without a word while looking back at Judy and shuts the door in my face. That's the last time I ever see Judy. I don't know, nor will I ever know, what happened to her. I just know that living and working in this place has driven her mad. I wonder if cornered by Miss Loftus she has been forced to face the weakest part of her, an admission all too much for this unfortunate girl who needs a safe place where she can rest and restore whatever confidence and psychic stability she has lost.

Yet all of us have similar challenges because of crowding and our never being able to easily get down the side rails of beds and then find cranking up beds or getting a patient onto and off a gurney equally hard. Feeding patients too sick and weak to help themselves, I too often find patients who take forever to swallow the gruel I'm feeding them and then the gruel usually dribbling down their chin and I have to start all over again. But one student in my class doesn't mind feeding patients, while I don't mind cleaning them if they make a mess. So we trade. I clean up her patients and she feeds mine. One small obstacle removed for both of us, yet we have to deal with the frequent incontinence of patients, none of us having dealt before with anything like that dirty job cleaning them, especially if patients are obese and helpless and we see frequent bedsores after not fully recovering from seeing others, one even with maggots.

I also witness a *paracentesis*, a treatment procedure involving an abdominal tap with a long needle used to remove fluid from the abdominal cavity to relieve abdominal pain and fluid buildup when several liters are removed. No surprise when one student feels faint and is helped onto a chair. The patient receiving treatment holds my hand so I won't collapse.

On top of all that, we are required to meet the challenge of always showing respect for doctors by our having to stand when a doctor enters the room or following him when he enters or leaves, even those from the South who are openly racist.

Thus we face the overwhelming demands of time and energy placed upon us as new students when we don't know at the time that the hospital relies on us because RNs refuse to work at County due to the low pay offered and the challenging conditions in which they would have to work. Yet while dealing with such continuous day-to-day horrors along with the shock of working on extremely crowded wards filled with very sick and usually elderly patients, we sometimes are offered incidents that will linger a lifetime:

The delighted thanks we receive when offering alcoholics paraldehyde, a burning liquid they love because it relieves their DTs, calms their shakes, and gives them an immediate, glorious high.

An alcoholic who has gulped so much sweet, cheap wine he has flies circulating his mouth he apparently doesn't notice or doesn't care.

An elderly man crying because he doesn't want to be cremated.

The expansive area of houses surrounding the hospital we can view from windows on upper floors, that area furnishing many of our patients, one whom by chance I meet one night at a bus stop when my father refuses to give me a ride all the way back to the hospital.

At the end of a long, hard and exhausting day on the wards, Linda, Zan, and I usually go to the library. We don't go to the library to study, although we do study a little or at least we pretend to. We actually go to the library to check out our "dream intern," Dr. Schneider. And while he isn't exactly what we consider handsome, Dr. Schneider seems sexy, perhaps because we spend most of our time with old and derelict men. Yet, out of all the doctors at County, we judge him by far the best looking, and he soon notices we are peeking at him over our books. In response, he seems quite amused as well as vain. So we nickname our favorite doctor, "Sweet, snooty, snippy, snappy, snazzy, sexy Schneider."

No surprise we don't learn much at the library during our first months in training, but we enjoy our studying Dr. Schneider who will never know how much he helped us get through those first grueling months of training. At least we could look forward to our evening trips to the library to gaze at Dr. Schneider who we think secretly studies us perhaps brightening his day or at least offering him a good laugh.

During September and October, my first two months in training, 1 am dutifully going back on weekends to stay with Babu and Aunt Jessie and Johnnie and working on Saturday as an elevator operator at the May Company Wilshire because I really need the money since $30.00 a month I'm paid by LACGH is barely enough to pay for books and clean uniforms, and I also have nowhere else to go. Sitting around the hospital on Saturdays and Sundays with no money seems dull, and I, unlike Linda, am not interested in meeting guys. Yet, as my relationship with Babu grows more and more hostile, weekends are becoming increasingly more miserable. My grandmother is losing her grip on me and she knows it. Always possessive, Babu can never let escape anyone she feels she can control. I know somehow I have to get away. I have to be one of the few who breaks from her grasp.

Finally a plan evolves. After three months in training, Linda and I are able to quickly make beds, give baths, pass trays, feed patients, so we decide to use an agency that places aides where needed in hospitals such as Kaiser, Cedars of Lebanon, Good Samaritan that are informally associated with County. At these private hospitals on our days off from county, we care for patients who have private rooms and a pleasant environment in which to get well. How different from County where our patients are jammed together in an environment that reeks of feces, urine, old age, and death.

Given the opportunity to earn money and escape Babu on weekends, I stop going to Babu's altogether. As a result, I even decide not going there for Christmas. During my final visit, I tell Aunt Jessie that there is lots of money to be made over the holidays working as an aide. Then I gather my courage and admit the truth. I tell Aunt Jessie I don't want to return to Babu's house on weekends because I am just too miserable while I am there. Aunt Jessie surprises me by becoming angry at my decision and tells me I am selfish and ungrateful for all Babu has done for me.

"Babu's not well," Aunt Jessie explains. "This might be her last Christmas. You can at least spend her last holiday at home with us!"

This is the first time I can ever remember Aunt Jessie being angry at me and so lacking in understanding of how I feel, but then I understand she is Babu's friend, not mine.

Aunt Jessie continues: "I know life with your grandmother hasn't been easy, but she did take you in when she didn't have to and raised you. She could have just let you go live with your father, and, believe me, that would have been as difficult if not worse than it has been here with Babu. Your father's mind is all tied up in plays and movies. He would have had no time for you!"

I am shocked! Aunt Jessie suddenly sounds just like my grandmother! I have always trusted that Aunt Jessie would support my decisions and help me stand my ground against Babu. Maybe her sudden change in attitude is due to Babu no longer being well and strong. Whatever the reason, my relationship with Aunt Jessie has also changed. No longer can I look to her for her support or her help.

The growing rift between Aunt Jessie and me as well as escalating problems with Babu make me understand that my real home is now at County, my new friends have now become my family, and while I feel sadness and loss, I also feel relief and a sense of suddenly being free.

But within a few weeks after my previous visit, I begin to feel remorse that I don't try to help Aunt Jessie at all when she is taking care of my grandmother when Babu is deathly ill from a stroke caused by her hypertension for which she is supposed to take medications but she refusing because of their horrible side-effects. When I go to visit Babu and Aunt Jessie after having not visited them for a long time, I find my grandmother lying in a pool of clotting blood and Aunt Jessie trying to clean her. The room is dark with the shades drawn. I help Aunt Jessie clean Babu and remake the bed. I try talking to Babu but she is far too sick to talk or even listen to what I am saying. From what I have experienced at County, I see clearly Babu is dying. Sad to say, I don't go back again to help Aunt Jessie with her terrible task as caretaker.

Not long after my visit, Babu dies. I don't feel guilty I wasn't there with Babu when she was dying. I feel very remorseful that I was not there for Aunt Jessie when she needed me. I do attend Babu's funeral but don't want to because of what I felt so strongly for my grandmother, and after Babu's funeral well-attended by all her followers and widely noted because of Babu's connection to Mr. Grey, I see very little of Aunt Jessie, and later, I won't remember our last visit or my ever having visited both Jessie and Johnnie.

I know that Aunt Jessie was excluded by Mr. Grey and my uncle from receiving any part of my grandmother's estate because Aunt Jessie was only Babu's friend. But I believe she should have received a larger inheritance than I did because she was such a devoted friend to my grandmother whom I ignored when she was dying because I disliked her so strongly even though she had done a great deal for me. I know without doubt my feelings of guilt about the last days and hours of Babu's life will not diminish. I will probably feel badly about my selfish neglect until I myself get sick and die.

Babu having become successful and somewhat wealthy on her own, Mr. Grey wanted her money and property when she died. He convinced her on her death bed to change her will leaving everything to him and his son Uncle Ned and leave me almost nothing. Mr. Grey suddenly re-appearing as she lay dying and his attention during that painful time apparently rekindled or finally offered the love that she once might have wanted from him, and Babu bequeathed to him everything that should have come to me and to Aunt Jessie who had been a loyal and loving friend for years.

Babu left him beautiful linens, beautiful gold-edged wine glasses and blue glasses for champagne. She left him fine furniture and rugs she had woven herself. She left him her spacious Dutch Colonial home and her several properties in San Clemente that even in those days were worth a fortune. [In an email, Paula Strahm reports that when she and her daughter drove by the house where Joan had lived with Babu, they found that the lovely Dutch Colonial house had been torn down and replaced by a nursing home.]

Mr. Grey took everything, repaid well for his years of having to abide Babu's insults and her physical abuse. I was so young I didn't understand what was going on, and even if I had understood, I wouldn't have known what to do, having no advocate, legal or otherwise, and my father certainly not wanting to get involved in that mess, so in the end I received only 500 dollars. I don't know if Aunt Jessie even got a dime. Probably not. That experience in business was a tough learning experience. I never did really recover what I should have received had my uncle and my grandfather been honest and decent. But they were greedy and from them I learned a bitter fact of life. I learned that you need someone to help and defend you and not someone who will steal all you have. I also learned that such a true friend is hard to find.

Mother always said that you were lucky if you could count your friends on one hand. She certainly was right, and if Mother would have lived, she would have made sure I had been treated fairly, especially since she surely would have inherited all the wealth that Babu had labored to earn.

A greater sense of loss than from my being disinherited, I will never know what happened to one of the two most important people in my life, Aunt Jessie who still accepted me even when I was disloyal to Babu. If I wanted to find her today, I wouldn't know where to look. I feel just as terrible that I didn't stay in touch with her and never knew what happened to her. Perhaps she went back to Saint Louis, although there was probably nothing there for her. Perhaps she and Johnnie finally lived together in some sort of life without my grandmother hanging on to Aunt Jessie for dear life and trying to totally possess her as she did everyone else.

Did Aunt Jessie end up in a resident home for the elderly? When did she die and where? I can't answer any of these questions and I feel shame after all Aunt Jessie did for me after Mother died. Without Aunt Jessie, I don't know if I could have survived living with my grandmother. Aunt Jessie always very patient and kind must have at times disliked Babu as much as I did because of the stranglehold of my grandmother's possessiveness. Someday I would like to find out what happened to Aunt Jessie and Johnnie, but I don't even know their full names. They both were my make-believe aunts, and during my childhood that was all that mattered to me.

After years of absence from my life, just prior to Christmas and his birthday, Dad suddenly comes to visit me at County.

Rubin Moskovitz (not a good name for the movies), then Romeo Romero (he got teased a lot about that name), and finally Ramon Romero, was born on December 25, 1905 in Jacksonville, Florida. Someone later for some reason began referring to Ramon Romero as having Basque heritage, perhaps because that origin rather than Slavic was more acceptable, more romantic, more suitable for the make-believe film industry he was involved in one way or another throughout most of his life.

I never met Dad's mother. Dad's father lived for a time in a room he rented from my dad. During that time, we called him Mr. Moss because of his manner. Mr. Moss and Dad never spoke, not even exchanging a greeting. Mr. Moss would arrive home from work, go directly to his room, and stay there the whole time until the next morning when he went off to work. My father had a brother (Antham) and a sister (Roxie). I never met Roxie (she died young) but I was fond of Uncle Antham who always quiet and helpful seemed the opposite of Dad,. He, unlike my dad, continually went to doctors for one ailment or another.

Dad always resented being born on Christmas Day because no one ever considered celebrating his birthday. Dad around 50 when I start training at L.A. County, of Romanian-Jewish heritage, with brown eyes, black hair worn a little bit long for the crew-cut 1950's, 6ft. 2in., underweight for his height, and skin tone the hue of olive oil he donated to me, he always dressed in a very casual style, usually wearing sandals with socks, and rarely wore a suit.

Dad, a handsome man who because he was an actor could change his appearance to fit a role, once played an American Indian, a priest, a lawyer, and an outlaw. One time he seemed to play all of them at once.

Estranged from me for years after Mother died, during that time, Dad wrote the screenplay for *City Beneath the Sea*, the highest grossing film in Hollywood for 1953, but while he earned a lot from that screenplay and bought two properties from his earnings, one in the Hollywood Hills the other in Echo Park, both neighborhoods considered dangerous at the time, especially the one in Echo Park, when I met him again, he still looked as poor as ever. Always an eccentric because he was so extremely frugal, you would never know he had any money even though as a smart business man, he made some good investments and managed to live off residuals from that one very successful film released in 1953 and lived on those residuals along with part time promoting of events at Hollywood Bowl until his death at 75 in 1980.

Zan now a steady friend who always has supported me through difficult situations helps me again with Dad whom I haven't seen in years. One day, I'm in my room talking with Zan when the old prison guard housemother comes to tell me, "Your father is waiting in the Acute Unit lobby! He wants to see you!"

I am totally shocked, suddenly afraid. My grandmother had always told me that Dad was an evil person and I should stay away from him.

I look at Zan with obvious fear, "I don't want to see him!"

Zan takes me by the hand, "I'll go with you. I'm sure everything will be fine."

Zan and I go across to the Acute Unit lobby. I feel like running back to hide in my room, but Zan won't let me. At first I don't know what I'm going to say. I don't know how I feel or how I should feel. I just know that I'm very fearful and hesitant after the fear and hatred Babu has instilled in me against my father.

I see Dad. He looks every bit as anxious as I am, maybe afraid that I will refuse to meet with him. He reaches out to me.

"Hello, Ramona," he says quietly and gives me a hug. I with hesitation awkwardly hug him back. I introduce Zan, and after exchanging a greeting with my father she leaves. I look after her as she descends the wide thirty-two stairs at the entrance to the hospital and strolls across to our residence.

Dad and I sit on a bench. Patients, doctors, families are strolling past us talking about their own lives. I at first feel very fearful and hesitant. No wonder after the fear Babu instilled in me.

He tells me that he finally felt he could come see me now that my grandmother had died and I was living at the hospital. Dad and I look at each other and we don't know what to say. I don't know how I feel or should feel. Finally, Dad offers:

"I've kept track of you all of these years, Ramona. I thought it was time for us to get together. I'd like you to come visit me and bring your friend." Then with excitement, he adds, "I want you to meet the dogs! "You'll love them!" (Little do I know then that all those dogs have fleas.)

I flush with sudden anger. "Why no cards! No calls! Not even on my birthday!

He answers quietly sounding remorseful: "Ramona, I just wanted to avoid a nasty custody battle that would only have hurt you. You know how your grandmother and I always fought each other so bitterly. I thought it best that I stay out of your life altogether until it was safe for me to contact you."

We talk at length about Babu and how she tried to destroy Dad's marriage with my mother and destroy our relationship. He asks me how I've been over the years since we last saw each other. I think of the time I saw him with his dog, I waiting for a bus when he hadn't seen me and I had decided not to speak to him and got on the bus and left him behind just as he had done to me.

I tell him how much I missed Mother, how I had given up everything that I had been doing while she was alive, quitting the Hollywood Professional School, stopped playing the piano, even stopped writing poetry and plays. I had just buried myself in my studies. I decided to become a nurse, so I read everything about nursing, Babu, of course, violently opposed, mostly because she didn't want me moving out from under her control and she thought I really could do better than becoming a nurse.

Having wrestled with my anger and sadness, finally through our sharing with each other our years apart, I begin feeling better seeing Dad again, and I agree to visit him before Christmas and celebrate his birthday a day or two early since I am planning to work over the holidays. Dad and I set a day and time for me to visit, and he gives me some convoluted directions for getting to his house where he lives with his pack of dogs some place up in the Hollywood Hills.

The next week, Zan and I go to Dad's house, but we have difficulty getting to his house when we try taking what Dad says is a shortcut to avoid the long winding street up to Dad's and instead climb a steep trail off Mulholland Drive, our often having to grab onto scrubs to pull our way up. When we finally reach Dad's place exhausted, his house looks like a shack in Appalachia even though in the Hollywood Hills. Realtors today would advertise my dad's place as "rustic," in other words, a dump, his filled with old books and a ton of papers. Dad a hoarder who never throws away one piece of paper, not even old receipts, his place is always neat despite being filled with old books, although he never seems to dust.

Dad loves used book stores, so his house is filled with old books, and because Dad is in the entertainment business, he spends a lot of his spare time attending movies and plays when he isn't writing them, so he also loves collecting old movie posters as well as clothes and jewelry used in films that he gives as gifts to friends and to me. I think it hurts his feelings because I with good reason never wear any of the clothes he gives me. Some dresses and hats from period films would have made me look more than a little silly wearing them, especially when I went back to County after my visits with Dad. Decades later, contemporary current culture would allow such make-believe apparel to appeal to many and would be worn openly with delight.

Zan is shocked seeing the place with its shelves of dusty books, stacks of old magazines and newspapers, scores of coo-coo clocks all ticking in unison and suddenly announcing the hour at the same time. Dad is a "bohemian" with friends who are artists and writers, and I'm sure he lives very differently from the people in Salem, Oregon where Zan spent her childhood and where her parents still lived.

Dad does his writing in the basement. You can look through lattice windows and see Dad typing. Arriving at Dad's place, we peer through the windows off the patio.

"Who's that?" Zan asks seeing the wild-haired man pounding away with two fingers on a typewriter.

"That's my Dad!"

As soon as Zan and I settle from our climb up the steep trail, I notice a portrait photo of a beautiful woman on his desk. According to my mother, Dad had quite an affair with a well-known Broadway star who had signed the photo "Dear Ramon, I know you will always be successful in everything you do. Love, Julie." Mother was rarely jealous, but she was of that woman.

When I ask Dad about the picture, he just says off-handedly: "Yes, of course, everyone who meets Julie loves her. She's such a fine actress." But although Dad acts quite causal about his knowing that woman, according to my mother, their friendship was more than causal.

Eventually my dad actually went to the dogs who became his only true companions. Starting with Sherif, a small cute dog of Heinz breed, one of fifty-seven different varieties, he soon had more and more dogs, and as a result, more and more puppies. One good thing about those little guys: they were great watch dogs offering 24/7 security. They would bark up a riot if anyone came near Dad's place which was at that time in an area of the Hollywood Hills considered dangerous. But I know from what he said on occasion that Dad got lonesome sometimes living alone, so the dogs always were great companions.

After visiting Dad, my typical days as a Probie on the wards drag on while I bathe patients, assist them in their oral hygiene, and give them backrubs. But there are other incidents that I come to know as somewhat typical of County:

My nausea viewing for the first time a *decubitus* ulcer so nasty I could see right to the bone while being told somewhat matter-of-factly that the patient had most likely developed the ulcer because of neglect from someone not having turned the patient at regular intervals.

My naive but well-meaning behavior for which I could have been expelled when I allow a lonely patient for whom I feel sorry keep a cockroach he had named "Willy" as a pet and feeding it crumbs in a drawer. The head nurse is furious when she discovers my misplaced sympathy, shouting at me that I have used terrible judgment allowing a cockroach to contaminate the ward and put all of the patients in danger of infection. She orders me to kill Willy, an act I find very traumatic. I am certain she will write an incident report indicating that I should be expelled, but when I report for duty the next morning, she says nothing about the incident. I go to the patient to say that I am sorry for having killed Willy. "You can't trust anyone," he mumbles, then turns away from me and faces the wall.

The head nurse on the Diabetic Ward we always will remember, a tiny black woman with reddish hair and a commanding personality. Interns are afraid of her because she knows considerably more about diabetes than they. One time when I wait while an intern writes orders, she grabs the chart out of his hands, crosses out his orders, and writes her own! The intern looks shocked, but he doesn't say a word, looks at me, and without comment hands me the chart.

After Dad visits me at the hospital and I visit him at his place, I experience another inquisition by Miss Loftus. She begins by asking me for a report about my experiences on the wards. I offer what I consider an honest evaluation by stating that I find them exhausting but inspiring and I confess finally understanding Babu's disgust with nursing but that the challenges I face each day has made me even more determined to succeed.

I surprise her by revealing my sudden reunion with my dad and how I have begun resolving the feelings I had toward him because of Babu's open hatred for him. I briefly consider revealing to Miss Loftus my going with Zan to Dad's house but decide against telling her because I know that she will be probing for a soft spot trying to destroy any defenses I might have about visiting his home for the first time after having been living separate from him for so long.

Instead, we talk about what Miss Loftus considers my "odd" living arrangement with my dad and mother while I was a child. Loftus claims something wrong or troubling about such an arrangement and tries to get me to agree with her.

I tell her I think the arrangement had been fine with fewer quarrels. I tell her about Hollywood couples having an East coast/West coast arrangement. But according to her, such Hollywood situations on principal were very destructive for children.

Miss Loftus tries again to get me to discuss my difficult relationship with my father. I recall what my roommate warned and what I experienced in our last session, so I am careful what I say. Loftus asks again what had happened with my father. I tell her again that he left after my mother died and I hadn't seen him in years.

I also reveal how Babu was so horribly possessive of every one who was important in her life, especially her immediate family and close friends, trying with a strangle hold to keep all of us close. I confess that since I had no easy way to get away from her, I finally went off to nursing school, my uncle drowned his anger at her in alcohol, Aunt

Jessie just put up with her as best she could, and Mother died. The only person my grandmother couldn't and didn't want to possess was my father. Babu would have liked to crush him and throw him to the sharks he said where always circling him. Babu thought Dad responsible for my mother's death. She claimed, rightly so, he never contributed a dime to my support or pay my mother's medical bills even when he had money. She claimed he had got inside my mother's head controlling her every move and that Mother obeyed him to help him fill his desires. Babu too often complained that I looked so much like my father instead of my mother, but Babu also prevented any connection I had with him, tried to destroy any connection, and almost succeeded until fortune took a turn when she became ill.

Miss Loftus breaks into my thought. "So your father has reappeared in your life. How do you feel?" she demands. "Do you still hate him? What would you really like to say to him? How would you expect him to respond?"

How should I answer? What should I say? Dad and I seem to be slowly dealing with issues from the problems generated mostly by Babu and her possessiveness.

Miss Loftus surprises me by observing quietly, "You still must be very angry at your parents who both abandoned you."

I angrily fight back. "My mother died because she wouldn't take her meds, not because she wanted to abandon me, and Dad is back in my life!"

Miss Loftus says nothing and studies me while I fight to control my anger until I finally sigh with acceptance. "Mother truly believed that through Christian Science she could heal herself and that medical science was useless. My dad was devastated by Mother's death. Before she died, he tried convincing her to take the new meds for TB that had just been approved, but she refused. Dad even threatened to divorce mother, as if that would somehow get her to listen, but she still clung to her faith in Christian Science, and as a result, one night she started vomiting blood, and she died alone. Dad told me he avoided seeing me to avoid an ugly custody battle with my grandmother."

Miss Loftus continues to study me as if she is waiting me to continue. What does she expect me to say next? But I only return her gaze, push myself from the chair, move to the door, and leave.

Loftus surprises me by not asking where I thought I was going or ordering me to stop.

Because I was not only my mother's child, but her best friend and confidant, my mom told me everything. From her I learned a lot about life, although I didn't understand much of what she told me until I was older and in training to become a nurse when I finally understand my father's preferences at a time when public attitudes required hiding even the slightest suggestion of homosexuality, and Dad certainly was not detached from life in anyway.

A "Hollywood type," he was always drawn to handsome men and beautiful women and they to him, and after Mother's death, he seemed to want someone, man or woman, who cared as much about plays, films, and writing as he did. My father did much of his writing in collaboration with his friend Harriet, but she was very different from Dad. I have no clue how such two different people got together, let alone work together. Reasonable, practical, and pleasant to work with and be around, she had a very positive influence on my father. I wish I could have witnessed their discussions, more likely battles, when they were developing the story ideas for their plays.

Yet no matter how close my father was to anyone, he never remarried after the death of my mother. As his only child and because I hadn't see him for years, some of his friends were quite surprised when they met me for the first time. Some even remarked that they had never been aware he had a daughter.

While he also had several male friends he met through his work in show business, he always had one friend who was more than just a friend. For a long time he was involved with Barry, a handsome man from Argentina. Barry had a girl friend Penny who always seemed unhappy, and Penny had a blond Cocker Spaniel that was crippled and dragged her legs behind her, so they seemed a perfect match. Barry was never nice to Penny and he kept Penny around just to prove he wasn't homosexual, a preference during that era dangerous to admit, let alone display. Most homosexuals in Hollywood at the time had wives, girlfriends, and even children to cover up their true sexual orientation, a trend that lasted until the advent of AIDS.

I often wonder why Barry was so mean to Penny. I recall one time at Dad's and we are on the patio when Penny carries in a six pack of beer for Barry who takes the beer and stacks the carton in the frig.

"Hey, Ramon, how come you don't have some food in here! You can't live on cigarettes and water! You for sure are going to die a slow death from starvation!" Barry returns from the kitchen, "Here, Ramon, you want a beer?"

Dad never drinks alcohol or takes any kind of medication, not even aspirin but does smoke incessantly, something too many were doing at that time.

Dad shakes his head. "And you're going to die from too much beer, Barry."

Barry never offers Penny a beer. Every time she tries to speak, Barry yells, "Shut up your mouth, Penny!"

So although Barry in a typical discussion he often has with Dad in which he claims he is Roman Catholic, from his treatment of others, he is obviously not a good one. Not only does he not love his neighbor, he obviously doesn't care for Penny.

Dad, a skeptic regarding all religious belief, especially Christianity, keeps asking, "Where is heaven, Barry? Show me! Above us? Below us? Where is God? No one is coming to get us and take us to heaven or purgatory or Hell or save us from ourselves."

My father never curses. Whenever he is disgusted or disagrees with someone, he yells "Baloney!." If people foolishly put up a fight for their ideas, Dad just keeps saying "Baloney" until they finally give up. So when Barry keeps coming back at Dad with some nonsense about believing being better than not believing or why take the risk that there is no God or salvation or you can't always have clear evidence for what's beyond our senses, Dad keeps exclaiming "Baloney! Baloney!"

Finally Barry gives up and starts talking about going to Santa Anita racetrack since he and Dad love horse racing. As miserly as he is, Dad always has a little "fun money" to "bet on the ponies" at Santa Anita.

We're all sitting on the patio except Dad. He's pacing back and forth as usual. Barry is having a cold beer and Penny is drinking water. Barry is reading the sports page outloud about the next major horse race. Dad and Barry talk about which horse they're likely going to bet on and the odds of winning. Penny listens attentively. Dad and Barry decide where and when they're going to meet. Dad asks Barry to pick him up as Injustice IV is not always running. Dad's dog Sherif hears something next door and starts to bark loudly. Barry looks annoyed.

"Come, Sherif, Sit!" Dad orders. The dog sits at Dad's feet. Dad pets his dog. It's easy to see how much he loves Sherif. Dad suddenly remembers I'm sitting there.

"How about you, Ramona? Would you like to go?"

"I wish I could, Dad, but I'm buried in school work. Got to write a care plan on an old guy with congestive heart failure probably related to his heavy smoking."

I look at Dad who is breathing thick clouds of smoke adding to the smog. "You've got to stop, Dad."

Dad gives me a dirty look that tells very clearly: "Be still, child! I'm your father! Don't tell me what to do!"

Penny who looks as beaten down as ever finally asks "Can I go?"

Dad who likes Penny starts to answer, "Of course!"

But Barry looks at Penny as if she's psychotic then blurts out in his Argentine accent he has been trying to conceal to gain roles in movies: "Since when have you suddenly become so interested in horses?"

"I've always liked horses," Penny admits. "They're so beautiful!" A rare look of rapture brightens her pale blue eyes that always seem sad.

"For Christ's sake!" Barry yells. "We are not going to Santa Anita to see the pretty horses! We are going there to make some money!"

Jamie, the crippled dog, suddenly has a bad attack of diarrhea all over the patio. It smells awful – even to me who has cleaned up too many attacks of diarrhea.

Barry looks like he's about to vomit. "This is exactly why I do not want to take you anywhere with that damn dog, Penny! Clean up the mess! It stinks!"

"Shit always stinks!" I say to myself quietly.

Dad looks sorry for her. "Penny, there's old rags under the kitchen sink."

Penny rushes into the house.

Barry has a nasty look on his face. "This is why I hate dogs! Especially Penny's dog, all crippled up like that!"

Penny emerges from the kitchen with wet rags and a paper bag. She looks anxious.

Barry sneers at Penny. "One of these days, I am going to take your dammed dog to the pound and let them put that crippled thing out of its misery!"

Penny looks like she's about to cry. She keeps cleaning the deck.

I find very hard not going over and slugging Barry's pretty face.

Dad is starting to get angry. "Come on Barry! Let's not make a big deal out of this.!"

Dad looks at Penny. Dad loves animals, especially dogs. "It's OK Penny. Jamie couldn't help it."

Dad looks directly at Barry. "Mark Twain has a great line about dogs, Barry. 'The more I know about people, the more I prefer my dog.'"

Barry shoots back, "Well, Ramon, now that we have talked so much about dogs, can we maybe get back to the horses?"

Penny finishes cleaning up the deck and Jamie's rear end. We all sit in silence.

"I've got to go, Ramon," Barry says. "We can decide what we want to do about going to the track later."

Barry hands Penny his beer can and pushes up from his lounge chair. "Come on Penny, lets go! Maybe we will have time to stop at the pound!"

Penny looks terrified. Barry winks at my Dad.

"Don't worry, Ramon. I am not going to do anything to Jamie – at least not today."

Barry, Penny, Jamie, and Dad all leave the patio and start up the stairs towards the street. Penny says goodbye to me, and Dad says he'll be right back.

I take a deep breath in relief. I'm with Mark Twain. The more I know Barry, the more I prefer any other animal!

When Dad comes back, I ask him, "How can you put up with Barry? He's so nasty and such a jerk!"

"We've been good friends for years, Ramona."

"Some friend."

Following months of training at County, we finally achieve Capping. Dad is in the audience looking very proud and handsome wearing a dark suit, white shirt and tie, and dress shoes, but he is with Gary, another of Dad's friends whom I don't like because he acts too effeminate.

Dad has many friends, especially women friends who adore him. Because Dad has always been good-looking, especially when younger (aren't we all?) as well as intelligent and talented, many women were readily drawn to him. I especially remember Harriet who was sensible and down-to-earth and with whom Dad often collaborated on writing plays. I also recall Maxine who looked like an old, forgotten movie star with long bleached blond braids. Although Dad was at times demanding and cantankerous, women cared about him anyway.

Dad tended to be a "romantic." He based his view of love as he portrayed it in the movies or plays he wrote where he dramatized love affairs through conflicts and problems between lovers that are happily resolved at the end.

Following the capping ceremony, I rush to meet Dad expecting to be taken out to celebrate just as the others who are excitedly joining their families and leaving. Instead, Dad informs me that he and Gary have tickets for a play, and then they leave and I'm left standing alone among the crowd of other students with their families and friends. I feel deeply wounded.

Zan witnessing that I'm about to cry comes to the rescue as always by inviting me to join her family, and although I still feel sad, I am glad to do something to celebrate the most important day in my training so far.

I don't sleep much after I get back to my room after celebrating Capping with my friends. I feel so angry. I feel so betrayed. Why would he choose Gary such a little weasel of a guy before me? Dad might have at the very least tried getting a ticket for me so I could have gone along to the play. Still angry in the morning, I call Dad and fake a cheerful attitude to suggest we meet for a belated celebration at the little Mexican restaurant in Hollywood we always have gone to before. At least that might be neutral ground.

At the restaurant, once we settle, order, and are served our food, Dad seems his usual talkative self in telling me about the play that he and Gary enjoyed seeing, but I am not responding to what he says with my usual interest. Instead, I am staring at my black beans.

Dad finally notices my lack of response and demands, "What's the matter with you, Ramona!"

I raise my head and glare at him. "You really hurt my feelings, Dad. Yesterday was my special day! You knew that! Last night I was looking forward to celebrating with my family like all of my other friends were going to celebrate with theirs! But instead you just leave me standing there by myself while you go off to a play with Gary!

"Ramona, you should be grateful that I came to your ceremony. I bet a lot of fathers didn't bother. At least I was there."

Dad's remarks make me even more furious. "You left me alone once! How could you go off and leave me alone again!"

I once again feel the rage sprouting toward my dad that Babu had so successfully planted. I can't eat. I don't want to stay here with him. I have nothing more to say. He had spoiled one of the most important days of my life to go to a play that he could have gone to anytime, and he had gone with someone like Gary!

I drop my fork, toss down my napkin, push back my chair, get up, grab my purse.

Dad appears angry, really angry. His eyes are blazing. "Ramona, if you walk out that door, that's it! I have had it up to here!" Dad puts his hand to his throat.

Customers and restaurant staff begin feeling the volcano of emotion that has been asleep for a long time and is now rumbling to life. I stand for what seems forever. A part of me wants to sit back down. Another larger part of me is too proud and too angry to sit and try to resolve our differences. My inner turmoil takes over my reasoning. I turn and walk out of the restaurant.

On the bus I take home to the hospital I feel sick. I had hoped that we could make up for the years we had lost, but I feel now that won't happen. Dad had his chance and blew it. And now so have I.

Dad and I don't speak to each other for several months after that incident. During my busy schedule, every time I think of Dad I again feel very hurt and very angry, and knowing Dad, he is probably feeling bitter, as he can't understand why I am so upset over the Capping incident. After all, he had shown up, and that was what he had been required to do.

I had learned through experience from witnessing incidents involving Babu that Dad tends to hold grudges against people for a long time, sometimes forever. I, my father's child, am not very forgiving either. No surprise, we are a lot alike.

Our months of probation at County lasting until we get our caps in June, 1955, before Capping we Probies live in a modern building and share a room with another student. I unfortunately have a Senior as a roommate whom I dislike. I can't remember much about this modern building and not much about the foyer except we dislike the housemothers who give us trouble every time we enter or exit the foyer of the student residence, one housemother we learn without surprise who had worked as a guard at the Tehachapi Prison for Women. Both search our bags when we leave for the weekend to make sure we aren't stealing anything from the hospital then search our bags again when we return to make sure we weren't bringing in illegal drugs

Following Capping, we live until our 1957 graduation in one of a row of two-story structures with surrounding chain-link fencing for security. Our living quarters are referred to as cottages but look like World War II military barracks and most likely are where the only decorations we can afford will be posters we tape to walls. We call our cottage secured by chain-link fence Virgin Villa, the unfenced residence for staff RN's referred to as Menopause Manor, and the quarters for new interns Shangri-La. Each of the six barracks have two stories with a wall phone and a corkboard at the top of the stairs for pinning messages with phone numbers.

The Psychiatric Unit across the street from our barracks faces Marengo. On the other side of Marengo, the Mortuary School where students have plenty of corpses to work on. Across from the Mortuary School on a side street, a convenient taco stand offering nursing students great tacos we can afford on our meager monthly pay.

To get to our classrooms and the wards, we have to climb a flight of stairs located at the rear of the hospital where much to my chagrin while still a Probie I act as Miss Professional Standards, a post to which I am elected and a task I hate having to inspect each and every student including my friends for clean uniforms, clean shoes, white hose with straight seams, clean fingernails, hair up off of her collar, and what we call our dunce caps in the shape of a cone pinned correctly to hair. Because I am Miss Professional Standards, I, of course, have to look perfect at all times, so I am greatly relieved when we get our school caps and I no longer have to perform that hateful task.

At the start of my Junior year in training and several months after the restaurant incident where I blew up at Dad in response to his dismissive attitude toward my receiving my cap, I start to feel remorseful from what happened and what it had done to our always fragile relationship. Zan, always helpful, suggests I call him, but when I do, Dad hangs up when he hears my voice. These hang-ups happen several times over several weeks. So I write him letters and send him cards saying I am sorry for what had happened, but I receive no response. Then one day I get a package without a return address. Upon opening it I am shocked to find that it contains all the letters and cards I have sent him, everyone of them unopened! I have no idea what to do next. I am crushed and feel like crying. Seeing my eyes welling with tears, Zan urges me to go to Dad's house and talk with him directly, a suggestion very difficult for me to consider.

"I can't do that, Zan!" I cry. "Dad is obviously still very angry and hurt with a grudge he probably might hold as long as he lives!"

I begin to feel even worse about what had happened, yet both Dad and I had said things we shouldn't have said. He should have considered my feelings about what he had done at Capping, But knowing my dad, he really did feel that he was doing a lot just by coming to the ceremony. Dad is often well-meaning but too often very self-centered, if not just down right selfish. He understands well the feelings of the characters that live in his mind and his plays, but he finds hard understanding the emotions of ordinary people struggling with their own feelings in the actual world. But with Zan's continued urging, I finally get up enough courage and decide to go face the fire-breathing dragon in his lair.

I know that Dad sleeps late after working all night, so I start to make my hour-and-a half bus ride to his place at around noon. I feel anxious not knowing what is going to happen. If this attempt to restore a connection fails, then I can do nothing more but wait and hope he forgives me just as I have forgiven him for those years I feel he had abandoned me.

The day I venture out to confront Dad is typically L.A. with temperatures before noon already hot, the air hazy with smog and smelling of ozone, a mixture I have come to recognize as typical. I recall heavy rains we experience usually in February that make the dry concrete trough of the so-called Los Angles River look like a real river. [14]

Santa Ana winds every summer finally calm, smoke from fires in canyons and forests finally clear, and we usually have a sunny Christmas. So because of our once proclaimed good air and endless sunshine, people from all over the country pour into L.A., but then due to the increase of more vehicles, air quality becomes worse and we have smog that becomes thicker every day until rain clears the air offering dazzling skies that attract even more people rushing to fulfill their ideal of California dreaming.

The first few times we have smog people exclaim, "What is this stuff?" We soon find out that "stuff" a stew of exhaust from vehicles, smoke from industry, dirt from endless construction, and early morning fog from the ocean, a noxious combination that greatly increases the incidence of respiratory illness we treat more frequently at County.

For my trip to Dad's, I catch my first bus on Morengo after a long wait. I look around at others on the bus, typical East L.A. people: Mexican mothers with several small children, homeless Gringos, all poor people who have collected enough money to ride the bus to County for whatever treatment they can pay.

Three young Latinos get on, sit all in a row on the bench seat behind the driver at the front of the bus. I can feel the rising tension among the other passengers. These guys obvious gang members (probably 17 or 18) have the exact same tattoos on their forearms that signify their gang. These gangbangers don't say a word. They don't look around. They just look straight ahead through the window across from them. Just what are they looking at? Their territory? Were they looking for members of other gangs? All I can view out of the window are scores of old houses and derelict buildings. When the three gangbangers finally get off the bus, all the remaining passengers seem to sigh in relief and again start chatting.

After what seems a dozen stops, I get off the bus and wait for the next with no place to sit and no shade, just hazy sunshine through smog and stifling heat. Finally, the next bus arrives. The passengers are different from the last bus, people from downtown: secretaries in light, flowery dresses and hose and heels, a few young business men trying to save money riding the bus, shoppers lugging bags stuffed with purchases. From where had they all come? Where were they all going? What unexpected event would happen to one of them today that could change their lives forever? An accident? A death? I wonder if anyone else is facing what I'm facing, a confrontation that could end the most important relationship in my life. Why did bad things seem to happen so fast – an accident, a violent crime – while good things always seem to take too long to develop – graduating from school, raising a child, writing a play.

I get off the second bus and finally board the third that goes to Hollywood by way of Rossmore Avenue passing the stately houses I admire so much in Hancock Park hoping that someday I will live in such a home. I view strolling girls from Marlborough School, rich kids in current fashionable uniforms of white blouses, short, mid-thigh skirts, white socks and loafers loudly squabbling with each other about their totally boring school and their totally boring parents and their totally boring lives.

Once we reach Hollywood, I study the crowd filing onto the bus: Tanned young women imitating Marilyn Monroe or Kim Novak with bleached blond hair wearing low cut blouses, all eager to break into Hollywood, eager for glamour and glory, all these sad little girls wanting and waiting to be discovered, suddenly becoming movie stars, gaining fame and wealth. What do they know about show business and the film industry? Absolutely nothing about how tough it is here, how lonely it is, despite the thousands of young people who feel they have been fortunate to come to Hollywood but have no clue that so very few are chosen and even those not lasting long. Eventually they'll be on a Greyhound heading back to Nebraska, Iowa, or Wisconsin with only memories to show for their sojourn out West to the world's most famous fantasyland, its name in towering white letters on one of the hills toward which I am slowly moving.

I get off the bus on Hollywood Blvd and see a Marlon Brando look alike trying to look sexy in a torn t-shirt, his fake attitude full of bravado and arrogance.

I decide to take the trail off of Mulholland Drive to Dad's even though it's difficult, but the idea of trudging all the way up the long winding street to Dad's place seems worse. I want to get this confrontation with Dad over quickly. Yet, the trail is so steep I again have to grab unto shrubs and pull myself up.

When I finally reach the large cactus that indicates the border of Dad's property and I end up on the patio, I feel hot, drained, sweaty, and tired. Am I ready for what I expect? I can hear the dogs yipping. The back door to the house closed, I see Dad through open latticed basement windows typing away with two fingers on some project. I watch him for a while, the ever-present cigarette burning in an ashtray on his desk. I finally get up courage and try to get his attention.

"Dad?" No answer. Daddy?" No response. Dad keeps typing. "Dad!" Dad still typing.

Finally "What do you want, Ramona!" Dad doesn't even turn his head to look at me. He just keeps typing.

"I need to talk with you, Dad. I've called you, and you wouldn't talk to me. I've written you. You haven't even bothered to read my letters. I finally decided to come see you."

Dad finally stops typing and looks at me. There is almost no expression on his face. "I have nothing to say, Ramona. I think we've said everything there was to say at the restaurant." Dad takes a drag on his cigarette and goes back to typing.

"Dad, I really want to talk with you! It's important to me! I've missed you! Please come out so we can talk!"

"I'm busy, Ramona. Go sit out on the patio if you want, but I'm going to keep working. I've got a lot to do."

"I'll wait out here, Dad."

Dad doesn't answer, so I turn back onto the patio and sit and wait. I know Dad will have to come out eventually, but I wish he would hurry! The umbrella over my head does little to protect me from the broiling L.A. sun.

I look out through the haze at what was once a beautiful view now with smog so thick I can barely see the city. Today, the cactus on the hill looks particularly dry and thorny. I can smell the noxious fumes from all the cars that jam the so-called freeways.

After what seems a long wait, I feel like leaving. But I won't. Dad's stubborn, but so am I. Besides, he caused the problem between us, not me. My angry words at the restaurant certainly didn't make the situation better. But I was angry from his dismissing as unimportant my receiving my cap, not even as important as some play he could have seen another time!

The basement door finally opens. Sherrif and Toto race out to me begging for attention. Dad sits down in silence, he picks a cigarette butt from the ashtray on the table and lights it.

"You know, Ramona, words are not like bubbles. They can be like bullets. Once you say them you can't take them back. You have to live with what you've said."

"I know that, Dad! It wasn't all my fault. I shouldn't have said what I did. I'm sorry! But you shouldn't have done what you did either."

Dad doesn't respond and I don't want to start another fight. I look at him:

"You know, Dad, I'm the only child you have, and you're the only parent I have. You and I, we now only have each other despite whatever so-called friends we might have who will eventually return to their own family and their own lives. So you and I need to get along and try to understand each other and help each other in anyway we can for the rest of our lives."

I expect Dad to accuse me of sounding as if I were a character in one of his plays. But he just looks at me for what seems a long time and then nods

"Yes," he finally answers and stands stretching. "My god, it's hot!" he sighs. "I'll get us some water.

Dad returns from the kitchen with a bowl of fresh water for his dogs, then goes back and returns with ice water for us that tastes really good but doesn't begin to quench my thirst.

"Thanks for the water. This must be the hottest day of the year!"

"It feels like it!"

He takes a long, slow drink of water. He looks at me. His eyes have come to life again.

"By the way, there's a new musical in town. Got great reviews! I have free tickets. Want to go?

"Sure! Sounds great!! I feel relieved. The crisis between us has passed as if the problem never happened. We're back in Dad's territory now, the one filled with plays, movies, musicals, everything he fully understands and that for him are certain and safe.

He looks expectantly at me "When? It's not going to be in Hollywood very long."

I look at my watch – my all important watch – large with a sweeping second hand – so essential for taking a pulse.

"I've got to check my schedule. I'm working extra as much as I can as an aide. Linda and I are working everyday we get off from County. We go all over to other hospitals. Kaiser's, Cedars of Lebanon, Good Sam."

"You're going to wear yourself out. I'm sure that dealing with County alone would be enough."

"I need the money, Dad! The thirty dollars a month I get from County isn't enough! Besides I learn a lot from what I do at those places compared to what I have to do at County."

"Like what?"

"That if you get sick, it's better to have money than to be poor like those patients we have at County where we give as good a care as we can given the conditions in which we have to work. I've learned it's better if a person has some weird disease no one has ever seen before and one we can learn from and the doctors can offer different diagnoses and try different treatments and make a name for themselves. I've learned that if you don't have unusual symptoms, you're just one more sick person to try to take care of or just another disease or condition to deal with."

I finally push myself from the lounge chair. Now that our differences between us seem somewhat settled, everything seems so much better: the city less smoggy, the cactus thorns less brutal and sharp, and I can hear the piano player at the bottom of the cactus covered hill start another lovely prelude.

But even though from my own study of the piano when younger I think the player sounds accomplished, Dad has no respect for the player's dedication and only complains that he is sick of hearing the same piece played over and over.

"Practice, Practice, Practice! That's all he does! Too afraid to get out and audition. Someone might say his playing is lousy and he will be crushed, never touch the piano again, and become a salesman!"

"Why don't you stop by and introduce yourself sometime when you're going out to get dog food?"

"Why waste my time on someone who has no imagination, no drive, no guts! This is the world of hard knocks! If you want to be a pianist, a writer, an artist, you'd better have guts! Lots of them!"

Dad speaks from his own experiences. My father a self-educated man with little more than elementary schooling ran away from home in Florida to New York City when 15 or 16. Working at menial jobs to support himself until he found a position as a reporter on a small local newspaper then winning small roles in off-Broadway theater productions, he later moved to the Los Angeles area and Hollywood where he became involved in early film production.

Despite Dad's persistent problems in the entertainment business (mostly due to his own stubborn refusal to change what he writes), he has never abandoned his dream of being a successful writer. He has no sympathy for a person who quits trying when life gets tough. His favorite saying expressing his contempt: "He's going to end up a traveling salesman!" based on the actions of the main character Willy Loman in the play *Death of a Salesman* who spends his life as a salesman. When he grows old, he loses his job because of poor sales, gives up trying to find a new direction, abandons his youthful aspirations, and ends a suicide.

We listen to the piano player begin again the same prelude.

"I've got to get going, Dad."

Dad gets up disturbing the little dogs at his feet.

"I'll give you a ride to the bus – that is if Injustice will start."

Dad has about as much luck with cars as he has with film people or race horses, mostly because he is too cheap to buy a vehicle that's dependable. My oldest memories of my father are of him frequently pushing his car to get it going. All of his cars named "Injustice," he ends up with "Injustice One," "Injustice Two," "Injustice Three," "Injustice Four," his latest.

"Thanks, Dad." Dad really has forgiven me! A ride!

We walk up the stairway together to the street. I look at the battered old car that is on its nearly bald tires. Maybe it would be better to walk to the bus stop. At least I'd get there.

Dad opens the door for me and gives me a hug. "I've missed you Ramona."

"I've missed you too, Dad, I really have."

He tries to start the car. After several of Dad's attempts, the motor finally roars to life in a cloud of blue exhaust adding to the smog. We move away from the curb and roll down the hill toward Hollywood Blvd.

My father loves Hollywood, the crazy people, the drama, the hopes, the tattered dreams. All would in some form end up on yellow paper in his old Remington typewriter. Nothing, absolutely nothing will ever drag him away from here – Dad's element, his home, his work, his life.

My father believed his two greatest achievements were: (1) having his play *Crescendo* produced on Broadway as *Swan Song*. [Paula Strahm in a email recalls seeing the play *Crescendo* written by Ramona's father in which Orson Wells played the lead and Ramona was the child star. Paula adds that Ramona had been signed to play a role in *Sentimental Journey* but lost the part when her mother died suddenly.] (2) Having written the screenplay *City Beneath the Sea* the year before I entered training, my dad's greatest failure was his inability to be a team player, an absolute necessity in the entertainment world. As a result of his not listening to others and being able to compromise, let alone relenting to the advice of others for revising what he had written, he lost a great career as a screenwriter for different Hollywood film studios, was blacklisted, and was never able to get another job in entertainment other than promoting Hollywood Bowl events.

Visiting him one time later, Dad refuses when I ask him to give me a ride back to the hospital at twilight.

"What! You want me to drive through that neighborhood in the dark!" But he does agree to drive to the Art Deco Macy Street bridge that crosses to East L.A. where he drops me off. "This is a far as I go! The last time I crossed this bridge when I was driving cab at night, I was mugged!"

"Thanks for the ride, Dad," I offer as cheerfully as I can.

I climb out of the car and start toward the bus stop as I watch Injustice drive away and grow smaller. Almost immediately a man approaches. What should I do now! I'm all alone!

But the elderly Latino who enters the circle of light from one of the lamp posts of the historic bridge surprises me by graciously addressing me by name.

"Miss Grey! What are you doing here! Walking around here is very dangerous, especially for such a beautiful, young woman like you!"

I greet him warmly, thank him for his concern, and explain to one of my former patients why I'm here alone.

"*Que lastima*! What kind of dad is that!" he exclaims.

"My dad," I reply in quiet resignation.

The man walks with me to the bus stop and waits with me until I get on a bus.

A very traumatic incident occurs during my Junior year. I'm getting ready to discharge a young patient getting ready to go home after orthopedic surgery, Leon, a young, strong-looking black man, twenty years old. I'm packing his clothes, and we are exchanging joking comments about our hoping to meet under more pleasant conditions when Leon suddenly places his hand on his chest and becomes extremely and increasingly agitated.

I yell for the Resident who comes running. Leon is trashing violently, and we use all of our strength to hold him down. He is struggling to breathe, his face contorted in terror.

Suddenly Leon lies still. A peaceful look comes over his face. As I watch this profound change, I see Leon first valiantly fighting death then just giving up as his soul takes flight.

Perhaps what I saw was a hallucination created by the trauma of my experience, but I still truly believe that I had seen his spirit leave his body. That image has remained my whole life along with my thought at the time as "his soul took flight."

I ask the Resident what had happened, and the Resident tells me, "Leon most likely threw a fat embolism that lodged in his lungs resulting in his demise."

And that was all, but as I go on with my duties that day as if nothing unusual had happened, I can't put out of my mind what had happened so suddenly and so unexpectedly to Leon when his soul took flight.

Most instructors and head nurses we work with on wards and in specialty services are helpful but expect a lot from us even though most of us are not even out of our teens and only students. Sometimes even attending doctors and Residents are helpful and supportive of our untrained efforts, but interns not so much since by the time we are in our second year of training we know more about working with patients than those interns fresh out of medical school who have just started dealing with the various challenges offered them at County.

Then during our Junior year while on surgical rotation, we have to work under the supervision of two circulating nurses of Japanese heritage who unfortunately for us at the time run the operating rooms and obviously hate us with a passion. We students all hate them in return. They yell at us in rage for the slightest mistakes. Yet, they are yucky sweet around the surgeons: "Yes, Doctor! Let me help you Doctor!"

Because there are two of these vicious nurses, we can never get away from them. They make our surgical rotation miserable. So before I leave on the final day when our surgical service ends, I ask Miss N, "Why do you hate us so much?"

She looks at me in disgust. "I hate you because when I was your age and should have been having fun, my family and I were prisoners in what was really a concentration camp! Born in America, we had done nothing wrong but we were Japs! When the war ended, we finally got out of that miserable desert camp and went home thinking we were going back to what had once been our beautiful, flowering gardens and green fields of vegetables only to find they were gone because we were forced to sell our land for whatever we were offered and someone had destroyed our gardens because we were considered enemies. I was no longer a young girl any more. I had lost my youth. You have your youth and your freedom! I was left with nothing! That's why I hate all of you!" Miss N. screams, slamming down a surgical instrument, glaring at me. "Leave!" she shouts.

I want to say how I understand how she feels and how sorry I am for what she experienced. Instead, I turn and walk away so relieved that I have finally escaped her control and her hatred.

I also recall clearly my very first day as a scrub nurse on OR Service. We had been preparing for this day for at least a couple of weeks. Our instructor, a beautiful woman with dark hair and eyes, is as cold and as sharp as the surgical instruments she is teaching us how too handle. When she judges us finally ready to scrub, all of us are afraid of what we are about to face even though we don't dare show, let alone voice, our growing fear.

The first surgery I attend is a Billroth II, a very complex operation where the greater curvature of the stomach is connected to the first part of the small intestine.

I scrub and stand by the operating table, my hands wrapped in a sterile towel. The patient is brought in on a gurney and transferred to the operating table. The surgeon and nurses then attempt to push a tube down the patient's throat. As the patient struggles, I start feeling faint. I tell my instructor, and she gets me a stool and tells me to "Sit down, take a deep breath, and don't faint."

After more preparations, the patient is anesthetized and the surgery begins. As I stand up, I look up at the big clock on the wall, and I guess that this surgery is going to take hours. I am so nervous I hand the scalpel to the surgeon blade first. I ask myself: "Am I going to live through this nightmare!"

I look across the table at the highly respected attending doctor. To my surprise, he winks at me and very subtly begins to point out the instruments for which the surgeon will be asking.

When the surgery finally ends after four hours, the head surgeon who performed the operation looks at me with admiration.

"You did a terrific job! You should definitely consider going into surgery!"

During my Junior year, I also meet a student who hates nursing, a Senior with whom I am working on the Women's Medical Ward. She has a full head of blond hair, a sweet, beautiful face, and looks like an angel.

We are cleaning an incontinent obese woman who is lying on her side facing me. The Senior doing the initial cleanup looks at the woman's soiled backside with disgust and states loudly what she's thinking:

"These big, fat, filthy old bitches make me want to vomit! I'm sick and tired of cleaning their shitty butts!"

The patient looks up at me. I can see the hurt in her eyes. I don't know what to do, and with the Senior standing right there, I don't know what to say to the patient or to her.

But when the Senior and I are finally in the utility room washing our hands, I have plenty I want to say.

"How could you talk about that patient the way you did! The look in her eyes! She was almost in tears!"

The Senior stops me with a smirk. "You're just a Junior! Wait until you've been here as long as I have! You'll hate these fat, old bitches as much as I do! My back's broken because of cleaning up their shit! I have only six months to go until I can get out of here! I will be so thankful! I can't wait!"

I note the two black stripe on the side of her cap that we younger students are working so hard to earn. How could a person like this graduate from my school? How has she fooled the instructors for so long?

I glare at her. I can hardly contain the anger that is continuing to surge inside me. "If you hate nursing so much, why don't you get out of training now! Anyone can see how you feel about patients! I bet you wish they would all die so you wouldn't have to bother with them anymore!" Then I feel a sudden need for revenge. "You know what? I'm going to report you!"

She fakes a laugh, her bright, blue eyes sparkling. "Report me? Me? You've got to be kidding! The instructors all think I'll be a wonderful nurse. They will never believe you. They'll just think you're jealous because I'm better than you and a lot prettier."

She pushes a few loose strands of her blond hair under her snowy white cap. "So go ahead, Grey. Report me. See how far you get."

She grabs a paper towel, carefully dries her hands. and with a wink and a sweet smile, walks out of the room.

Several weeks later, assigned alone to feed several senile old women on the 18th floor, a long dreary ward, I'm dragging along a cart with bowls on it and a hugh pot of soup brought up from the basement kitchen 18 floors below. Greta, the first woman I try feeding, I can't get to swallow. Oh well, she will have swallowed by the time I' get back to her after I feed the others. In the meanwhile, I can hear Millie hollering in the background. She's in restraints for a good reason. She's screaming over and over, "Get me out of here!"

The next patient looks at me with deep resentment and closes her lips tightly. I put a spoon of soup to her mouth. She seals her lips even tighter.

"Come on, Sally. Open your mouth. You have to eat. If you don't eat you'll die."

I know what Sally's thinking. I'd be thinking the same thing if I were in her place. "I'm going to starve myself."

The next patient Violet is very obese. I smell the familiar stink of feces. I look at her turning chart. It's been over an hour since she's been turned. She's been lying in her own feces for an hour. I visualize what's happened beneath the sheets. I can see the development of a bedsore. After I feed everyone, I'll have to get help, come back, clean her up, roll up her bed, and try to feed her, try to keep her alive. For what? Who cares anyway? No one.

I've got to rest a minute before I go back to deal with Millie who's still screaming, "Get me out of here!". I lean against the wall beside the window on the 18th floor and look out at the pigeons. Pick, pick, pick. They've found something to eat. I look into the distance at a beautiful sunset. Lots of red and orange. I've heard sunsets are more beautiful now because of smog. What a strange but typical exchange.

Enough rest. I'd better get going. I dish up soup for Millie and go to her bedside, crank up her bed, my back breaking, and lean over the side rails to feed her. Thank god she's restrained.

Millie looks at me and smiles what seems a sweet smile. Well, maybe she's not as bad as I thought. Millie opens her mouth, I give her a big spoonful of soup, but instead of swallowing, she suddenly spits it at me hitting my chest. My once white uniform is spotted with soup. Millie looks gleeful.

Oh Shit! I take a napkin and try to wipe it off. My uniform stinks. I'm so sick of this. Is there ever a day—just one day—that I don't get spit at, someone vomits all over me, or I clean up shit!

A young woman whom I've not seen before suddenly calls out to me. "Help me, please help me! Get me out of here, please!"

How did she end up here on Geriatrics?

I read her chart. "Caroline, I'll do everything I can to get you out of here as soon as I can. Right now I have to finish feeding these others, then I'll go to Admitting and see what happened."

When I finish feeding the old women as much as I can or as much as they will take, I go down to Admitting and find it typically jammed. I locate the head nurse on duty. I explain the situation of the young woman on Geriatrics and ask for help.

"I'm really busy, Miss Grey," she replies wearily. She looks bitter as she surveys the crowded room. "Why do these people always wait until evening to come in at the same time!" she says loudly with disgust. "They have all day to come in, but, no, here they are now on my shift! Half of them are senile! Most don't even know their names! The other half can't speak English! They've lived here for twenty years and haven't bothered to learn the language, so I have to find an interpreter and then...! She throws up her hands in despair. "Oh, don't even get me started!"

I know she is frustrated, but I have to press her further. I visualize Caroline on the edge of her bed, crazy with fear from the scene of senile women old and dying that surrounds her, she praying for me to get her out of that hell hole, waiting and waiting and waiting for me. I gather my courage and ask the head nurse again.

"Miss E, when will you be able to arrange for that young woman to get off Geriatrics?"

"Not now, Miss Grey! And probably not this evening! I'll have to go to the administrative office to get her transferred. I'll take care of it as soon as I have time!"

She glares at me and I know I'd better not push her further. She starts leafing through a chart.

"Promise?"

"Yeah, sure, I promise," she mutters. Then she again surveys the admitting room and something catches her eye. "I gotta go!"

She hurries away from the desk toward a woman who appears about to vomit.

"Carlos! Where are you! This woman needs a pan!"

An orderly rushes out of one of the rooms towards the woman who is starting to vomit.

I leave the admitting room feeling that the head nurse for Admitting may do nothing.

A day later, or maybe two, Caroline, the young woman trapped on Geriatrics, is finally moved to another ward.

Working on Violent Women while a Senior, I have a bad experience similar to what I once read in the *Nun's Story*. I am taking care of a patient in leather restraints who wanting a puff of a cigarette begs me and sweet-talks me into releasing one of her restraints so she can smoke. I light the cigarette for her, and she viciously tries to burn me. I am totally shocked. I call for help to get the cigarette away from her and get her back into her restraint. I stand humbled by the reprimand from the head nurse while the patient listens with a self-satisfied smirk. That day I learn not to ever trust psychotic people, no matter how sane they seem.

During my rotation on Violent Men Ward, I also have a surprise contact with someone whom I have not seen in quite some time when I'm informed that my uncle has asked to see me. I'm dismayed but not surprised when I'm told where to find him.

Ned Grey (Nejelco Dragamanovich), my uncle and Mother's half-brother, was my hero during my early years: He helped save me from Babu and gave me a direction in life.

Unc, like my dad, was very vain. He loved the adoration that he received from women. Tall, handsome and masculine with a good amount of sex appeal, Unc was also the eternal bad boy whom women so often love throwing their lives away trying to reform their man. Yet once evolved into a plain looking guy with balding head and sad eyes, these women — like Penny and her Barry — would no longer find him appealing. The good guys were those who held their marriage vows sacred. The bad boys always remained single even if they wore a wedding band on their finger.

Men also liked Ned, although they never did when he was drunk, which eventually happened to be most of the time. When he was sober, men liked him for his great sense of humor. He was also the consummate sportsman, especially great at fishing and tying flies, a skill that during one extended period of sobriety he built into a successful business. Unc in a lot of ways was a lot like Hemingway, his favorite author, a man's man, living in a world of hunting, fishing, fighting, drinking, writing terse prose that establishes a style for his generation and beyond.

Unc even looked a little like the great man himself, masculine, tough, fearful of becoming weak or ill, so afraid that, just like Hemingway, he, in a moment of despair at the thought of his impending future facing chronic illness due to rough living and hard drinking would consider taking his own life with his favorite shotgun so he would never have to face old age, the loss of his mind, and his ability to see the world and express it in his own, special way.

Unc loved his German shepherd Dante more than anyone. I had to be very careful around Dante. Unc warned me to never get too close or make any sudden moves around Unc or my aunt. Unc took great pride in having trained Dante who would refuse to eat until Unc spoke a word in Slavic, and Dante would have died of starvation rather than eat without my uncle's permission. My uncle loved Dante so much because Dante loved him drunk or sober and accepted Unc no matter what he did. When Unc started drinking again, Dante was still there while Aunt Marge left and his other friends started to vanish from his life and then Dante was killed by a car.

Losing his last and only friend, Unc began to really hit the bottle hard ending on the Violent Men Ward at my hospital. Surprised he had asked to see me, I knew he had reached the last rung on the ladder down to the abyss, and it was just one more groping step before he fell.

Unc did love Aunt Marge who was a strong woman until she became addicted to narcotics thanks to a doctor who offered Marge boxes of syringes filled with Demerol advising her to use them to stop her chronic pain from kidney disease.

When Marge became an addict she totally changed. Once a self-controlled woman who was a reliable support for Unc, she became an irritable, angry individual who could think only about her next shot of Demerol, her spirit slowly dying becoming unrecognizable, slowly transformed from a person I loved to be with to someone I knew was lost to me and to my uncle. And when she finally left him and he lost his dog, he fell completely back into drinking.

Unc disliked Babu even though he also respected his mother as much as I did, but he disliked her more than admired her for the same reasons, her possessive stranglehold on anyone she thought she cared for, especially her last born, only surviving child, my uncle. She ruined his first marriage with her constant intrusions into his private life. Both my uncle and I knew that she had ruined my mother's marriage to my father.

Unc and Mother, his half-sister, were quite close, although she disapproved of his drinking and was saddened from watching him destroy himself and his marriage. Once during my childhood both my mother and Uncle Ned were in bad shape at the same time and my grandmother was stoically taking care of them both. Mother dying of TB was in one room, Unc was across the hall recovering from a bad auto accident that he had when he was drunk and at the wheel. I did feel sorry for Babu at that time. It was hard on her to have both of her children both so beautiful and so talented lying in bed, one deathly ill, the other gravely injured.

I don't recall talking much to Unc during that time. He certainly didn't feel like talking. He hated having to depend on Babu. Now she really had him in her possessive grasp and she could heap on him the guilt for what he was putting her through along with her having to nurse a dying daughter and raising a grandchild who should have been with a self-centered father instead of with her. Didn't she already have enough problems without having to deal with him too, an alcoholic son?

We both hated her possessiveness and Uncle Ned helped me break the chains that bound me to her. He told me that he had heard how tough Los Angeles County General Hospital was but maybe once I had trained there I would still have a chance at freedom from my grandmother. When Unc finally healed enough to walk on his own, he moved out and went back to Margie and back to drinking. The fact that he had almost been killed didn't matter. All that mattered was getting hold of another bottle and getting another fast car that he always drove too fast.

Riding with Unc was, of course, always dangerous but often exciting. He should have been a race car driver. He loved to drive fast. I remember driving with him up into the mountains and how he would speed up driving into a curve and how we would always come out alive. He owned one of the first MGs imported to Hollywood direct from England, a right-hand drive, bright green convertible. He loved everyone admiring the car and admiring him with his dark tan and stylish sun glasses. Some men did inspect me, but I assumed they were just admiring the car. I also loved riding with him because I felt as if I were with a movie star, everyone staring at us, especially women.

Unc was a great jazz man. He was a wonderful composer and jazz pianist. At the height of his music career, Unc played at the Tracadaro, the swankiest, most glamorous night club on the Sunset Strip offering the sort of glamour that was part of the mystique of Hollywood situated right below the Hollywood Hills where all the stars lived in their private palaces overlooking L.A.

Unc told me that he had started hitting the bottle heavily at the Trac. Patrons would come up to the piano bar, offer him a drink, and say, "Play it again Ned. Play it again" as if they were saying something original. So Unc would play a medley of songs and have a drink with everyone of them. Glamorous women almost draped themselves over the piano so they could be closer to my uncle, look into his eyes, and enjoy his amused smile they thought was just for them. And then they would offer him another drink, until finally, my uncle a chronic alcoholic dealing with blackouts and hallucinations finally quit the music business, went into the fishing tackle business, and stayed sober until his life fell apart around him, taking him with it.

A bad guy in several ways — alcoholic, womanizer, wife beater, my mother often got very angry with him. We'd drive past Margie and Unc's place. Mother would notice his car not at home. She knew him well, and guessed he was off having sex with some woman, most likely only for a night. Then he'd go home and slap Marge around as if she was the one at fault for asking where he had been all night. One time when we stopped by, Marge had a black eye and we saw that he had broken a lamp to hit her with or Marge had broken it in self defense.

I think that Unc really did love Aunt Margie and they had a good relationship when he wasn't drunk and she wasn't loaded on Demerol. But I did wonder if Unc or any man was really capable of love or even had any feelings at all. I never saw a man cry or really talk about his innermost feelings or his regrets or his dreams for the future. Unc struck me only as a male primate, far more interested in making conquests of women than loving them.

Women for him were objects, accessories to satisfy his male ego, and for a long time I did not know that men could feel, could care for and love someone other than themselves. What really seemed to matter was respect from other men, they more concerned with their buddies and their sports, mostly wanting to win through sexual conquest and war. Winning was what mattered most.

After Unc fell back into alcoholism, his views might have changed a little. Maybe he finally understood the importance of love and women as something other than objects. Or maybe he just became bitter while drinking more to dull the sense of isolation brought on by continuous drinking. He did stop drinking for a long time until Aunt Marge became so sick and an addict and she divorced him and his beloved dog was killed and Unc went back to the booze more heavily more destructive than ever until he ended up in the Violent Men Ward at County.

When I visited Unc that time, he told me: "You never lose the taste for alcohol – no matter how long you stay sober. And if you go back to the bottle, you end up a worse drunk then ever. The demons are still in force and you can't escape them. It doesn't take much to fall off the wagon – but in my case I was facing plenty – loss of Margie, loss of my business, loss of Dante. When I was in AA I did a lot to help others who were alone in the world stumbling around in some alley or in some jail, all of their relatives having deserted them at last in some desperate attempt at self-preservation despite the love for their son or daughter or father that they still felt at some deep level. But even if no longer drunks, they were still alcoholics – forever alcoholics – going every day or many times a day to their local AA meetings where they could reveal only their given name and confess they were an alcoholic. I've tried more than once climbing the AA 12 steps to where I would be clean and sober, but I've never made it to the top."

With lively, brown eyes, dark brown hair cut short Uncle Ned built tall and solid always looked great with his trimmed mustache looking like a real movie star reminding me a lot of Clark Gable –– flashy in a cool way, a head-turner for women. A very careful dresser, I never saw Uncle Ned look bad except when I saw him locked up in the Violent Men Ward at County where he looked horribly beat up with a black eye and scruffy clothes and hair that needed cutting and washing.

Unc looked as if he'd been in a big fight, probably in some bar. His favorite form of defense as if he were in a movie was to smash a bottle and go after his opponent with the jagged edge. Unc had been brought into Violent Men by police because of such a fight. By then he had no one to worry about him or take care of him. Aunt Marge was in Las Vegas going through her own life of torment because of addiction, and Unc hadn't seen his daughter from his first marriage since she was three years old, so he wouldn't even know her if she somehow suddenly appeared.

Uncle Ned was one of those alcoholics who could be extremely drunk, but unless you knew him really well you'd never guess he's had more than a couple of drinks, just good at hiding his habit keeping it in a closet filled with empty bottles. However, I could always tell when Unc was drinking. After Marge became a Demerol addict, I knew he was starting to drink again after years of being sober. I could smell the liquor on him and I recognized a change in his voice, his words ever so slightly slurred.

In my first year when still a Probie at County and Babu had become deathly ill from high blood pressure resulting in another stroke, the last time I saw her she was bleeding from every orifice. So I wasn't surprised when one day soon after my last visit to see Babu I found a terse note on the bulletin board in the foyer of my residence. "Your grandmother died this morning. Call your Uncle."

I called Unc right away. He having just started drinking again, the news of her death hit hard. As much as we hated her at times, her death was a blow to both of us, especially since Babu was the kind of woman whom we, her unwilling possessions, thought would bury us all and keep on going forever. I didn't want to go to her funeral because I felt so strongly from how she had treated me just because I reminded her of my father whom she wanted dead if she could somehow manage making that happen.

But Unc told me, "Ramona, you've got to go to her funeral out of respect. I resented her too and I saw how she treated your mother and how she treated you, but she is still your grandmother. She raised you when she didn't have to. She provided for you and my sister while your dad went his selfish way. I'll pick you up on Saturday at 2:00. We'll go to the funeral together."

Unc did pick me up in another of his flashy MG sports cars, but he had on dark glasses, so I couldn't see his eyes that were probably a bit puffy and red but not from crying.

"Where's Aunt Margie?" I ask.

"Margie isn't feeling well. Her doctor still loads her up with narcotics that helps ease her kidney pain a little, but then she always wants more and she's injecting herself full of Demerol all the time. If she doesn't get it, she becomes agitated and angry. I tried taking her box of Demerol away from her last night and she became so furious with me, I thought she was going to hit me with a lamp. I'm afraid she's born to addiction just like me. I felt like opening a bottle of booze I've not touched in years and drinking it straight down!"

"Did you, Unc?" I asked, curious that he still had a bottle so available.

"No, of course not!"

But I knew Unc was lying. I knew the cycle had started again from a clean, productive life of sobriety to one again ravaged by booze.

"OK, so I had a couple of swallows! So what? That's it! No more! I couldn't go through that hell again!"

"So what are you going to do, Uncle Ned? How are you going to get Aunt Marge away from her doctor?"

"I don't know? But right now we are going to your grandmother's funeral. That will be enough misery for one day!"

But I also knew that he had begun going to work late when he had once been totally consumed with his work, he and Aunt Margie working hard side by side building a successful fishing tackle business. Later, when Marge left for Las Vegas, he would miss days at work when he took to driving up into the mountains in his MG and sitting in his fishing boat with Dante out on his favorite lake.

Unc knew that in spite of all his problems, he had always been my hero, the opposite of my dad who was his own kind of hero, more an antihero going against the grain of society with his load of problems: wildly eccentric, handsome in a movie star way, bisexual, talented, artistic, but extremely selfish. Yet, as Mother always said: "At least your dad doesn't drink!" one hugh problem eliminated from all our lives, one tragedy that didn't destroy a whole family, too often forever.

When I visited him on Violent Men, Unc didn't want me to think of him as my hero who now had become a drunk again. I still felt something for him, but he again had become the alcoholic he had been, only worse.

As Unc used to say, "Every time you fall off the wagon, you hit harder than before until you finally hit so hard that you just lie in the dirt and you don't get up again. It rains on you, the sun beats on you, the sand at the ocean covers you, and finally you just die, buried there with the world grateful that you're gone, the streets less contaminated by one fewer drunk. Some people might grieve, but they also secretly rejoice having one fewer problem, one fewer sorrow burdening and darkening their lives."

When I saw him that time on the Violent Men Ward at County, he sounded bitter and sour and reeked of those same odors. His great sense of humor had vanished, leaving him drowning in self-pity. He had started to look puffy, his eyes red. I knew that he was physically and mentally sick, and I inspected him for signs of jaundice, a bloated belly, complaints of pain issuing from a man always stoic who had thought complaining unmanly and always laughing off pain and illness as a joke until Dante was killed and Unc finally hit bottom, getting into bar fights, street fights, fierce verbal fights even with his friends he started to lose one by one until he ended alone in the Violent Men Ward at County a broken, battered man.

Seeing him in that derelict condition broke my heart. But other than what I had learned in training, what could I do? I offered to be there for him, but he didn't want my help. He didn't want me in his life. He didn't want to be close to anyone. He needed to be alone and to sort out the overwhelming problems that had brought him to this fall from sobriety that had turned his life from recovery to disaster. He claimed that when he was released, he was going away somewhere to heal, become whole again, find another dog easier than finding people who didn't give a damn after all the misery he had brought into his own life and into theirs.

I didn't know what to do for him, so I left the ward without a word. I hate to admit that I couldn't stand seeing my once handsome uncle looking like he had been dragged down every back alley in Los Angeles. So after visiting him on Violent Men, seeing him a broken man with all of his close relationships severed, I knew I wouldn't see Uncle Ned or hear from him for a long time, so I admitted to myself that I didn't want to see him again, and I never did.

Aunt Margie had been a great person to be around until she became addicted to prescription drugs. She had helped me through the worst years of my life, those seven long hard years after mother died and I was left to suffer living with my grandmother. What a nightmare!

The day mother died, my grandmother was getting all of the attention, all of the hugs. I got a few "I'm so sorry dear about your mother." I finally went out into the rose garden in back to be by myself. Then I called Paula, my best friend whose birthday was the same as mine.

"Hi Paula, my mother just died and I don't know what to do."

I went to see Paula and she and I talked about death and our parents. Paula recently had unexpectedly lost her dad.

[Paula remembers Ramona calling her but because Paula's father had died unexpectedly two years before when Paula and Ramona were in the 6th grade, Paula completely broke down when Ramona called. Not wanting Ramona to know about her father's death and knowing a blubbering person on the phone would be no help, Paula told Ramona, "I can't talk right now!" and hung up. But Paula insists that she and Ramona talked later more than once about losing their parent.]

I'd been waiting knowing it would happen, but Mother seemed so well that I didn't think that she was really going to die, especially after the good time we had together seeing *Brute Force* starring Burt Lancaster the night before she died. The afternoon of the day that Mother died, Aunt Marge called and came to get me out of the house away from my hysterical grandmother. We went to a movie, a silly story about pirates and damsels in distress and wild sword fights, a swashbuckling type of movie my dad loved, sort of like *City Beneath the Sea* or the novels he wrote that were never published.

For some time after my mother's death, I spent a lot of weekends with Aunt Marge and Uncle Ned, most of the time while they worked in their fishing tackle shop. Unc and I made lots of visits to the Nisei women who worked for him. Everything went generally well until Aunt Marge's kidney disease got worse and the pain was almost unbearable. That's when she got involved with a doctor who gave her lots of oral pain killers that did little to stop her misery and then boxes of syringes filled with Demerol.

I tried to warn Aunt Marge that she would become addicted if she continued to take this poison, but she just became angry, accused me of not caring, of thinking that I understood her pain better than she did and that I thought I knew all about pain and suffering when actually I knew nothing. She soon became a different person, at first irritable or sullen, then angry and hostile. She wasn't going to let anyone take away her drugs including Uncle Ned whom she repeatedly reminded of his sordid alcoholic past.

And when Uncle Ned did begin drinking again, there they were, once a happy couple now turned into a drunk and a drug addict. One of the most bitter and sad memories I have had watching the decline and final collapse of two people I loved. And given all I had eventually experienced at County, I had seen nothing worse.

Early in my Senior year of training, I, as so many, struggle through a period of extreme burnout. One morning, I just cannot get out of bed. I have felt this sense of exhaustion coming on for a long time. I am short with patients, dread every day on the wards, and basically want to quit. Zan and Linda try to get me out of bed so I can see a doctor to get excused from duty, but I don't want to see a doctor who would grill me about what I had been doing to become so tired, as if he didn't know. And I certainly did not want to offer anyone a tally of my extra-curricular activities working as an aide at other hospitals, taking evening classes at East L.A. College, spending whatever brief free time I had with Rick, my boyfriend, whom I had met in a philosophy class.

My refusal to get up and report for duty with others having to force me out of bed develops from the overwhelming conditions we all had to endure: The massive hospital throughout the year without air-conditioning a hot, sweltering, overwhelming smelly stink hole, the horrific heat mixing with rank odors from feces and disgusting food, especially breakfast a runny porridge that looked more like vomit, our own meals in the cafeteria just as gross. After a while (for some, a long while) most of us became accommodated and hardly smelled the odors, so we didn't feel like gagging as we first did.

Yet some students never did get used to the noxious stench of the wards, and that problem, along with all the many other miseries we had to endure drove many in our class out of training seeking more tolerable situations at home or college or a more sane line of work, and by June, 1957 our class had only 56 graduates receiving diplomas from the original class of 130. [15]

In addition to my burnout, I have more than one painful physical problem that makes work on the ghastly wards even more difficult. Sciatica and painful feet make standing for long periods and walking miles of corridors exhausting. Sometimes I want to quit just because of the pain. But I get some relief from special shoes purchased with what I earn by working as an aide at other hospitals that, of course, requires extra hours of standing and walking. I also have a board under my mattress, as well as physical therapy twice a week for some time without which I would never have finished training. Years later I will recall the hot packs therapists put on my back and performing massage.

Linda, Zan, and I frequently give each other back rubs after we get off duty. Sometimes I think that there might be more to those backrubs than just therapy, but I don't sense our ever having any inclinations other those backrubs easing our pain and we just needing a bit of caring touch after having rubbed so many painful backs of patients who have gone through so many hard years of lifting and hauling and hard work. I think we just needed a little loving comfort ourselves or we could not have gone on. Besides, if anyone else, especially faculty, had learned of our practice, they would surely have raised questions about our sexual inclinations.

When I talk to my dad about my burnout problem while we share a meal at our favorite Mexican restaurant in Hollywood, he sets me straight as only he can about the grim realities of life and how he has often felt the same way but that he has always kept going anyway by doing what he feels he has to do. Dad never allows himself to wallow in self-pity although he can be bitter and angry and resentful about what life has dealt him. He tells me what I already know, that my working every single day in the midst of hardship, misery, and pain is not good. But then he tells me to stop feeling sorry for myself, think about other things than nursing, maybe do some writing, see a movie, quit all the other jobs I might have, and try to get some rest. He tells me to get up and get going and finish training and then do something different, something I really want to do just for me. He tells me he never gives up and neither should I. If I did, I would regret my failure the rest of my life. I would always remember that I had failed just because my life and my required tasks seemed too difficult during one time. He tells me that life offered no excuses, only reasons, and there were no answers at the back of the book.

During our Senior year, Jan McKinney writes a note trying to comfort a young woman in an "iron lung" who had contracted polio making her unable to breathe. Accused of being "seductive" (i.e. homosexual), Jan is threatened with expulsion from County. During the time I knew her throughout training, Jan was my hero. [16]

Originally from Saint Paul, Minnesota, Jan at the time of our training is 29, thus considered "old" by younger Probies, about as tall and as slender as most of us, but strong and able to do the heavy work required.

Just as the rest of us when not on duty, she dresses in skirts, blouses, sweaters, and sandals or oxfords, hose always with perfectly straight seams. She always very fussy about having a neat appearance, Jan wears only scant lip rouge and no other makeup.

Although an attractive person, Jan doesn't date. Divorced when she was 23 because her husband was an alcoholic, a condition Jan couldn't deal with, she has no children. One time when some of us are relaxing in the common room, I overhear Jan talking with older students about her former husband, claiming that she had loved him but couldn't deal with his drinking. The subject comes up another time when we are discussing how alcohol ruins our patients lives and the lives of their families. We also note how nice alcoholics are when they weren't drinking but can be very abusive when drunk. Jan reveals that because her husband became very abusive when drunk, she had left him and started college. As a result of a broken marriage due to alcohol, Jan doesn't drink and disapproves of our taking bennies from heaven before a test or Ritalin for energy before going on the wards.

Everyone likes Jan, and we younger students look up to her and other older students. Jan is a very intelligent person who likes to study and learn. Always very studious, having gone to the University of Minnesota before coming to County, Jan is a very bright person and excellent student. We younger Probies all respect her and look to her for help and advice during training. Jan is also friends with older students and nurses in their 30s.

Having attended the University of Minnesota but not graduating with a degree in engineering, deciding instead to take a practical approach required by current social values when women aren't accepted in a "man's" field such as engineering, Jan is working toward a degree in nursing (later completing a five-year Bachelor of Science program at USC), and with her engineering background, she is very good in all the technical aspects of her new field of study and knows how to deal with the more complicated equipment we use.

She often talks about becoming an OR nurse, and from working with her on OR service we all see she would be an excellent supervisor in the OR. Jan's character makes her seem very strong and hardworking and quite self-sufficient and self-reliant, something we younger women often desperately need when we are Probies.

Although we live on the same floor at the barracks, Jan and I are mostly acquaintances. We talk occasionally when we are in the common area doing our ironing or just sitting around talking and relaxing. We also discuss our too frequent bad experiences on wards, I especially always griping about the terrible conditions and the often questionable quality of our training.

Jan and the older students find my continual complaints amusing, especially when I go on at length about Lillian Wald, my hero whose brave work I admire in the slums of New York during an era when women didn't work outside the home at all unless they were nurses and even then were restricted to somewhat protected environments. One time in response to my excited praise of Lillian Wald, Jan responds by suggesting that when I graduate, I'd probably work in some dreadful, dangerous neighborhood where there are gangbangers and rats running openly in packs, and for awhile I think she might be suggesting that I would stay on at County after graduating and eventually after years of dedicated effort I'd rise to assume the position of the present director. But, of course, I have other goals that I never reveal to anyone.

Jan always serious, bookish, and not rebellious, someone we consider very "straight," certainly didn't seem manly despite her apparent strength but also not especially feminine, just a plain, hard working person. So we all are shocked when an instructor and head nurse falsely accuse Jan of being seductive with a female patient. In response to the threat of Jan's being expelled, the rest of us protest, our entire Senior class standing up for Jan and demanding to meet with the entire faculty in the auditorium.

Once gathered, we face the entire faculty and threaten to walk out even though we are Seniors. Miss Loftus glares at us and shouts at us:

"How dare you! Just who do you think you are!"

But we stand firm and Jan is not expelled when the faculty and director of the school back down to avoid further media attention the hospital has previously been attracting because of staffing problems and issues regarding the treatment of patients.

Later, however, most likely in retaliation for our protest, our entire Senior class is locked up in the psych unit over a weekend to find out who might be homosexual. How the staff might accomplish that has always been unclear since if someone were observing us 24/7, why would any Senior be stupid enough or brash enough to indulge in any behavior that might even suggest sexual behavior? No one in that class ever revealed any specifics of that ordeal, many deciding Miss Loftus must have been behind that peculiar event given her obsession regarding homosexuals, and some of us wondered outloud whether locking us in the psych unit without due process was even legal while it surely seemed perverse. Who was calling whom psychotic?

But despite all the uproar over possible homosexual behavior, a short time later I do something really stupid by taking a young psych patient off campus to a nearby park. A clear, sunny day, she and I walk to the park near the hospital. With no benches available, we lie on the grass, look up at the clouds, and try to see images. We talk about our childhood. We talk about the poetry we have written. We are just a couple of young women rather than a student nurse and psych ward patient.

Suddenly I realize in a panic how late it's getting. "We'd better get back to the ward right now!" And I know that I'm facing some serious trouble with the school so homophobic.

Back at the ward, the head nurse sends the young woman back to the treatment ward and calls me into her office. Both the head nurse and my ward instructor are furious that I've been gone so long. I respond to their inquisition honestly and opening:

"Where did you take the student, Miss Grey?"

"To the park," I answer quietly but afraid.

"Why did you go there? What did you do there?"

I tell them the truth about our lying on the grass and looking at the clouds and talking about our lives. They accuse me of being seductive, a charge I strongly deny. Both loudly state my behavior is not acceptable, that I need counseling, and they will report me to Miss Loftus.

I call Dad because I'm very upset about what has happened to me on psych service and how I have been accused of being seductive with a patient my age. Dad is so concerned he actually comes to the hospital in Injustice IV and takes me to a nearby Carl Junior's. While he eats and I sip iced tea, I tell him about the growing paranoia regarding homosexuality at the school of nursing. Dad tells me to watch my back because there is so much animosity against homosexuals. I tell Dad that I'm worried that the head nurse and instructor will tell Miss Loftus who will call me in and grill me about my sexual inclinations.

Dad tells me, "This situation sounds dangerous! You'll have to stand up against such threats! Remember, if someone tries to push you against the wall, you push right back! You've got to protect yourself!"

I tell Dad it's only a matter of time before someone – if not me—gets kicked out over a false accusation. I'm just waiting for the blade to fall.

One afternoon prior to my third meeting with Miss Loftus, I'm ironing a uniform in the sitting room of our barracks. Movie magazines and several newspapers are scattered everywhere. With newspapers and magazines available in the common room, we often discuss some of the articles we read. Norma, a Junior who is much older, maybe in her early 30s, is reading outloud an article in a local paper about a young homosexual who was brutally beaten to death in Hollywood, the article very hostile towards the victim and citing homosexuality as a disease and proposing possible cures that would violate an individual's rights.

I'm not surprised at the number of such horrible cases lately, especially in Hollywood and the Hollywood Hills. I think about Dad and his friends Barry and Gary and of Dad getting beat up or murdered and feel afraid for him, but how can I discuss with him my worry. He would only become angry and claim I'm accusing him of something that isn't true.

The others discuss the problem, but because I know Dad is bisexual, I feel very ambivalent about the subject, so I say nothing. Everyone in this school seems worried about being accused of being homosexual and possibly expelled.

One naïve 18-year old recent Probie from a small town in Orange County and very religious, asks, "What's a homosexual?"

The others smile and suppress their wanting to laugh outloud. Jean, currently working psych services, describes how such men locked in a psych ward for being homosexual appear feminine, how they take continual abuse from other psych patients who are supposedly normal, but then she adds, "Too bad they can't be treated and cured."

Norma says she knows at least two who have to live their lives in hiding out of fear even here in Los Angeles. I imagine what it must be like in Kansas or Iowa. I think again about Dad and Barry and Gary.

Someone raises the subject of the two students who have been recently expelled for appearing seductive. We talk about the fear of homosexuality throughout the training school and how homosexuality is considered a disease by the American Psychiatric Association, considered a sin by most religions, and judged as illegal and punishable as a crime.

Jean warns us: "We shouldn't be talking about all this. Miss Loftus wouldn't approve."

But during my third meeting with Miss Loftus, she surprises me by not asking me about the incident with the young psych patient I unwisely took to the nearby park. Instead, she asks me why I'm not more upset about the two students having been expelled from the training school for being homosexual when I had supported the protest against Jan McKinney being expelled. I reply that the charges against Jan were unwarranted since I wondered how writing a note of comfort to someone confined in an iron lung could be considered seductive.

While Miss Loftus is berating homosexuals, I think about Dad, and, of course, I don't reveal that I know Dad is bisexual. I'm sure that would make her day. I feel very defensive, but I can't show my real feelings to this woman. I feel angry when Miss Loftus orders me to read the description of homosexuality as a disease in the APA manual. She notes that I haven't completed my psych rotation, probably never have read the APA description before, and ends by insisting that homosexuality is a sin and a crime and homosexuals are often arrested for molesting young boys.

I again feel confused by what she claims. Is Dad really a bad person? Is he sick or psychotic? Will he get beaten up or murdered for being "queer," or is he simply an artist? So many artistic people have homosexual leanings they must keep secret because they are so hated by "normal" people and their sexual inclinations can become dangerous for them and result in beatings and murders.

Miss Loftus asks about my life in Hollywood, my parents who were in films, and did I ever meet any of my parents friends who were homosexuals? Then she shocks me further by asking bluntly.

"Is your father homosexual?"

"Of course not! I exclaim angrily. "He loved my mother! He was devastated when she died! I'm his child!"

I try calming myself

"I can show you his photo. You'd see how much I look like him. Same coloring, same Basque and Gypsy heritage, and I have a boyfriend."

"I see," Miss Loftus says, studies me, looks again at a file in my folder.

"So how do you perceive yourself as progressing in your training?" she asks.

Sometime in January or February with hard, steady rain outside Dad's basement study, I'm absorbed in a book by Freud on psychoanalysis. Dad asks me what I'm reading. I tell him I'm reading about defense mechanisms, and when he asks if I'm reading Freud for some class, I tell him about Miss Loftus and how she is always trying anyway she can to break down a student's defenses. This is the first time I have told Dad about my disturbing experiences with Miss Loftus, how she is making me doubt myself and everything I believe, and how she is always trying to destroy my confidence in finishing training and getting my RN and becoming a good nurse.

Dad looks at me with surprise. He obviously has had no idea of what emotional trauma I've been going through. No surprise since I have never wanted to offer him even a clue that might make him question my goals.

"What do you mean, Ramona? How can she make you doubt yourself? This doesn't sound like you. You lived with your grandmother too long."

Right! But where was he when I needed him after Mother died?

I tell Dad about Miss Loftus and her obsession with homosexuality and about the homophobia that permeates the school. I tell him how she constantly makes me and other students feel we are always in denial, or only projecting our problems onto other people, or rationalizing our denial, and she always insisting that we need to face ourselves and our denial no matter how painful. I tell him that she didn't believe I could make it through training, how she had disapproved of me getting into training in the first place, how she continues to insist I must hate my mother for abandoning me and I must feel guilty for Mother's death. I tell him that no matter how I deny what she accuses me of doing or not doing, I have reached the point that I didn't know if anything I thought about myself was the truth and I was just trying to fool myself. I don't, of course, tell him about Loftus trying to get me to admit that I hated him for deserting me or asking me if he were homosexual.

Neither Zan nor Linda seemed bothered by Miss Loftus who appeared to consider me especially troubled and seemed trying deliberately to make me miserable and full of self-doubt. Zan always appeared so "normal" and quietly confident, our counselor had little interest in Zan. Linda was always so rebellious and honest and open about her feelings toward her parents and life that Loftus apparently had little challenge and thus little interest in dealing with someone so fractious as Linda. I think I was just too different from other students having what our so-called counselor considered an unhealthy background, permanently damaged by my mother's death, my dad's desertion, and my grandmother's tumultuous, possessive behavior.

Having to deal with Miss Loftus was a nightmare for every student she considered troubled and in denial. My experience was especially bad because she saw me as damaged by my early life and the loss of my mother, not capable of completing my training with all of the stress that went with it, and not capable of being a good nurse if I survived training. Mother's death, indeed, was the biggest life-shaping event I ever went through and had a lasting effect on my life. I cannot talk about her to this day without crying.

Dad appears shocked at what I have revealed. "You can't let people push you around, Ramona! You have to be true to yourself! You know what you feel! You know who you are! You know that everything she is saying isn't true! She's the crazy one, not you!"

All the clocks suddenly begin coo-cooing at once all over the house.

Dad finally stops pacing and looks at me intently.

"Just who is this crazy woman!"

"She's the counselor for our school. She's supposed to be helping us get through training. What a joke!"

But I suddenly feel like crying.

"I don't know what to do, Dad! I hardly know who I am anymore! I'm so confused!"

I really can't hold back the tears.

"How do I defend myself! How do I protect myself and not get kicked out of school! This woman has so much power over all of us!"

Dad crushes out his cigarette and lights another. He remains quiet for a long time. He finally gives me one of his evil smiles that suggests he is about to offer a gypsy curse.

"Ramona, from your experience in theater, you know how to act. Just think back when you were in one of my plays. Remember how it felt? You were only playing a character. You weren't really you."

"So what are you saying? I should just put on an act?"

"Given your present peculiar situation, yes. And I'll tell you exactly how you will pull it off!"

Excited by the scene he has suddenly created, Dad goes to the refrigerator and pulls out pumpernickel bread, salami, and water.

"Want a sandwich?"

I decline and wait while Dad throws together a slice of salami and bread.

"First of all," he offers while chewing on his bread and salami, "you should begin thinking of the hospital as the setting for a play and your appointment with your psycho counselor as a scene in that play. When you open the door to her office, you see yourself walking onto a set with her desk, her books, the chair you'll be sitting on only as props for the scene you both will be playing. And when you begin your so-called consultation or—whatever it is – you are both just acting out your roles by speaking your lines. For this scene, you are playing the role of a frightened student nurse with lots of problems.

"Well, that won't be too difficult!"

Dad gives me one of his frowns.

"Miss whatever her name will be playing the role of an all-powerful counselor who is using the theories of Freud to intimidate and dominate you!"

"She certainly does that!"

"And she is playing her role to the hilt.

"Absolutely no problem for her doing that!"

"But because you are such a great actress, you really get into your role! You really do feel scared!

"I'm always scared, Dad!"

"And you really do believe everything she says!"

"But that's what I'm trying not to do!"

Dad stops to catch his breath, relights his cigarette and studies me waiting for my response.

"So you're saying that I should think of Miss Loftus as just a character in a script being played by some actress chosen for the role of a controlling school counselor whose feels she needs to intimidate students?"

"Yes, of course! Ramona, you're not that dense! You've been through the routine! Now you need to ask yourself: Exactly what is my role in this scene? A student nurse with problems for Miss Loftus to expose? A student nurse who listens to Miss Loftus and grows confused? A young student who is filled with fear by this counselor's accusations and afraid she'll be kicked out of school?"

"How about 'All of the above'?"

He waves off my comment. "But once the scene ends, you will get up and you will walk off that set, and you will no longer need to play a role. You will be your real self again, and you know that everything the two of you have spoken were just lines and that you both were just characters in a play, but you are now back in the world of real things and real people. So Ramona, just play the role and you'll be fine."

My final meeting with Miss Loftus is the first where I have not felt completely helpless. Armed with the technique Dad has suggested, this time I try to act less anxious and defensive than I have always felt when under attack. Following Dad's coaching, I begin visualizing her office as a set in a play, Miss Loftus as an actress playing her role of a controlling Freudian counselor, and I playing my role of a fearful, compliant student. I act as if I have finally come to understand that she is right about how I have been using my defenses, especially denial, to protect myself from facing my true feelings about my past and about myself.

And as I start playing my role, I suddenly understand that I have, indeed, been in denial. Miss Loftus seems pleased by my confession – as pleased as she could ever be. She appears satisfied that she has won by molding me into a limp, vulnerable person who absolutely no longer has any defenses.

She asks me about graduation just a few weeks away and if I felt ready to face the new responsibilities that I will face with my elevated status.

"Yes, of course," I reply as sweetly and as grateful as I can. "Why wouldn't I be ready after all I've experienced at County and survived, especially with your help?"

At first Loftus seems smugly self-satisfied by my praise, but then I can tell that she doesn't like that I appear so confident.

Miss Loftus tells me how much I have matured over the previous three years, but I still have a lot of work to do on my denial and that I still have some of that defensive attitude that worries her.

I know that I have to be careful now. I really need to play the role. In no way can I allow my real feelings show. So even though I want to gag on my words, I while smiling as sweetly as I can thank her for all the help she has given me preparing me for my life ahead. Then I know I have to get off "the set" before my performance starts going downhill, especially when I feel I might throw up.

When I go to Dad's place just before graduation, we talk about what I might do after I finish training. I notice again his shoddy furniture both in his house and especially on the patio. I also note Dad wearing his typical old tattered clothes always with a sweater vest and worn down sandals. I know that Dad has made lots of money from his movie.

"Dad? Why don't you buy some new furniture and clothes and go out to a nice place for dinner once in a while? You should have plenty of money from what you got from your screenplay."

"Ramona," he tells me, "writers must be careful! I'm only fifty-two. I might have to live on residuals for the rest of my life. Residuals suddenly get cut in half, then disappear altogether. That's why they're called 'residuals' because of the little that's left after all the big shots take their cut. That's why I'm investing what I can and not spending on a bunch of junk I don't really need!"

I know he doesn't need fancy food and doesn't need much. Pumpernickel bread and sausage is good enough for him. Dad is always talking about "The World of Hard Knocks," one of his favorite topics that is always the theme for one of his plays, but always including romance and adventure ending in ultimate good fortune for all those struggling against the world that batters them.

"Ramona, I've seen too many successful writers end up destitute because they weren't careful with their money. They thought their joyride would last forever. Well, nothing good lasts forever. Only the hard stuff, the harsh realities, they're always there just around the next corner ready to happen and take you by surprise."

I agree with him, of course, and change the subject by suggesting we go out to eat. As we climb the stairs to the street and Dad's latest model of "Injustice," I already know where we'll eat.

We climb in, Dad releases the handbrake and lets the vehicle roll down the hill and gain momentum before he lets out the clutch to start the engine.

"Dad? How many versions of "Injustice" have you had now?"

"Six or seven. Why?"

"Maybe you should paint the number on the door."

Dad snorts a laugh then gives me a dirty look.

"Honor they father!" he grumbles as we slowly coast downhill toward Hollywood Boulevard.

Once we settle in our favorite Mexican restaurant and order our usual, Dad exclaims:

"Your patients and the hospital offer such wonderful material for books and plays! You should start writing again!"

"I have started writing again, Dad, but mostly for my class in philosophy."

But I don't tell him about my writing on what now is referred to as feminism and my raging against the pejorative image of the nurse I have come to know as depicting a nurse as indentured servant or vamp or whore, a theme I will later use as the subject of my graduate thesis.

"That's not the kind of writing I have in mind. What happened after your mother died? Why did you stop writing? Before your mother died you once wrote such beautiful poems and really exceptional plays and stories for someone your age."

"I just felt so depressed after Mother died I couldn't write anything except what I had to write for school."

But then I think of the play I wrote after my mother's death in which everyone died by the end. No wonder when all I saw around me was death of young beautiful women from tuberculosis, one just 24 years old to whom I talked through a window screen of her bedroom and Babu and I used to visit her and tell her about my mother who had the same disease and was too sick to come with us. Then one day our visits to the beautiful young woman stopped when we learned she had died.

There also was another young woman, very beautiful even though in the last stage of tuberculosis. When she died her mother said to Babu: "I wish your daughter would have died and not mine." Understandable but cruel, even more so after Mother died soon after, and I have always wondered whether the young woman's mother felt better when she learned of my mother's death.

I tell Dad, "My belief in Catholicism helped me more than anything after Mother's death. Now I don't care about religion anymore. I just want to get through training and see the world."

"Be careful what you wish for," he replies with one of his favorite gems of advice.

"I know, Dad." And I help him finish:

"Because the world is filled with hard knocks!"

We both laugh as the waiter serves us our favorite dish.

Several days later right after my ward duty I use the wall telephone on the balcony of our barracks to call Dad a day or two after having received but not returning his call. Dad is angry with me for my not returning his call immediately. Because he is so self-centered, Dad expects other people to give him their total attention and loyalty. So whenever I am late in returning his call and I explain I have been busy with training and an evening college class and working as an aide in other hospitals, Dad says to me angrily:

"Ramona, I don't care how busy you are, you always make time for the people you care about!"

Unfortunately for all those he cares about, Dad rarely follows his own advice.

Dad informs me of the reason for his call: He has two passes to his movie that's screening in a theater on Hollywood Blvd. "You want to go?" But he doesn't ask whether I can given my schedule.

Yet when we go together to see *City Beneath the Sea*, while viewing the film, I see how imaginative Dad is and how I once was just as imaginative but somehow lost what I had when Mother died. Having lost everything I once loved, now I'm just down in the trenches.

But I consider what Dad advises. I need to start writing down my thoughts about what I've lived at the hospital and what I've experienced in the "City of Angels". OK, but where should I begin? Well, how about following the well-aged advice: Start with what you know. So I take his advice when I begin to write again, and I start with him:

Even though Dad could be worth millions, he would still live in what would appear to others as poverty. For example, my father refuses to spend money on food but loves horse racing and as miserly as he is, always has money to "bet a little on the ponies" at Santa Anita. However, his refrigerator typically contains a loaf of pumpernickel bread, a package of the least expensive sausage, a bottle of water. Once in a while, he goes with me to a Carl Junior's for a hamburger, or we share a meal at a Mexican restaurant on Hollywood Boulevard where we can get a great meal with a glass of wine for only $2.00. And as I too often have absolutely no money, usually Dad will treat me to dinner. Even he has to admit the place is cheap. But the food is good, so it becomes our favorite place for our favorite food whenever we meet and I can get him to eat out, a real treat for me after hospital food.

Unlike so many people at that time, Dad is not prejudiced against any ethnic group, or sexual orientation, most likely because he has his own blend of ethnicity and sexual preferences, so he has no compulsion to cast the first stone. Instead, he finds most people interesting, and he is always thinking about ways he can incorporate their personalities into a script for a film that will most likely never be produced.

Dad has very strong ideas about politics and religion. A staunch conservative believing in strong authority to promote the status quo and at the same time limit change, he takes an avid interest in all religions although he was raised in the Hebrew faith. Widespread prejudice against Jews in the 1950s, despite what happened during the previous decades might have been one reason Dad changed his name from Rubin Moscovitz to Ramon Romero. He looks Latino with his dark, handsome features, his coloring, his hair style, so his assumed name fits him perfectly, although his assuming a latino profile requires him using caution because of the prevailing sentiment against "wetbacks" in California, one reason why he began referring to what he claimed was his Basque heritage.

But because of his Hebrew upbringing, Dad could be "difficult" to live with. He was very finicky about what type of food my mother prepared, driving her almost to distraction by his insisting, most likely because of kosher custom, that different foods had to be served on plates that had a specific color: Eggs prepared following his exact directions had to be served on a black plate or he wouldn't eat them. And when in my pre-teen innocence I asked him why the plate had to be black, he replied with assured adult authority because that's the way eggs should always be served. But when I asked, "Why?" He would order me not to ask so many questions, and that I better not ask him why. To make things even more difficult, Dad was color confused (a trait he eventually passed to my son), so he saw colors differently than "normal" people. I apparently wise beyond my years had the good sense never to cook for him.

Dad always stingy with his time as with his money, his writing always came first. He said he needed peace and quiet with no distractions to do his work, so Mother and I lived with Babu, and we visited Dad at lunch time and on weekends. No one I knew could understood this unusual arrangement, but I thought it was normal. In show business, this practice was somewhat common. A husband who was in the movies would live on the West Coast, while his wife who acted in plays, would live on the East Coast. On occasions when husband and wife did get together they usually got along better. Mother and Dad because they didn't see much of each other rarely got into arguments as did other couples, and then they disagreed only about what roles in films he thought she should accept.

Always extremely hard working, Dad wrote plays, movie scripts, and for a time he was also a reporter. Whenever I stayed at his place, I can remember him typing on a script most of the night. And he always fought for what he believed in, no matter the result. Unless Dad totally agreed, he would not allow anyone, no matter how well-known or what level of authority, to change a single word of his writing. I often asked my mother:

"Can't Daddy go along just a little bit with the people he works for, especially the producers who have all the money?"

My mother always had only one answer for me: "You can criticize your father all you want, but he has the courage of his convictions!"

As a result, despite his talent and past successes, Dad so difficult to work with, always insisting that no one change one word of anything he had written, he finally was fired from a steady, well-paying job at RKO Studios, and in effect he was blacklisted in Hollywood, so for awhile he produced films in Argentina for which he wrote the screenplays and in which he acted. My mother had roles in several of those films, and that was most likely when they became involved in something more than make believe although equally romantic.

But despite his problems in the entertainment world of hard knocks, Dad never lets go of his dream of becoming a successful writer. He has no use for a person who quits trying when things get tough, and he expresses his contempt for those who seem to give up by exclaiming: "He's going to end up a traveling salesman!".

Dad has always had two different attitudes towards life. On the one hand, he seems the most bitter person I've ever met by his frequent use of his favorite line: "This world is one of hard knocks." But Dad made his life much harder than it had to be because he was so stubborn about his work when show business by its very nature is a tough business filled with disappointments.

On the other hand, Dad is also one of the most optimistic people I have ever known. He will not let life get him down for very long. If he doesn't receive a contract for something he has written, he will start immediately on a new project, and he stays enthusiastic about the new work until he far too often hits another bump in the road.

Yet he also has a great sense of humor. For that reason, people love to hear his wild stories about his life and work. If we are eating out somewhere, people at other tables always appear trying to listen to what he is saying because what he says so loudly with such flourish is usually so hilarious they join us in laughter.

Dad always a fighter never lets anybody push him around. Dad has always supported me if he thinks I am being unjustly treated. When wrongly accused of acting seductively toward one of my patients and I am facing the prospect of being expelled, Dad gives me one of his favorite pieces of advice: "If someone tries to push you to the wall, you push them right back!"

Another time Dad, who never drank alcohol, never used other drugs, but smoked nicotine incessantly, made the mistake of renting one of his houses to drug addicts yet somehow kept them under control by standing up to them and never losing his "cool" in quietly admonishing them to maintain his property, an attitude they apparently respected.

But Dad could also be obstinate in carrying a grudge, as he did against me for a long time after what happened when I asked my father to come to my capping ceremony. Dad's attending the ceremony meant a great deal to me. Capping seemed the most important event until my eventual graduation from County. Capping was the first immediate goal in my difficult training because of my having to overcome the doubts others had about my succeeding. When I looked out into the audience from the stage, and saw Dad there with a friend, I expected Dad and I would go out to celebrate after the ceremony as all of the other students did with their families. Instead, Dad told that he and his friend were going to the premiere of a play, and when I asked if I was invited, Dad said that he didn't have a ticket for me. So he and his friend just left me standing there by myself among a crowd of celebrants. I must have looked really hurt because my good friend Zan invited me to go along to celebrate with her family, her parents traveling all the way from Salem, Oregon to see their daughter receive her cap.

Because of that incident at Capping, I was very angry at Dad. He, of course, couldn't understand why I should be angry at him, no surprise, and then he, of course, got angry at me. We didn't talk to each other for some months, yet we were finally able to restore our relationship, although I was the one who had to seek him in his sanctuary and he at first didn't want to see me, so through my typical persistence, much like his, I was able to restore our bond.

What my father hates most in life is Christian Science, for he feels that my mother's fanatical belief caused her death because it preached no medications under any conditions. Despite the new life-saving drugs for TB having just been approved, my mother refused to take them. Dad even threatened her with divorce if she didn't take them, as if that somehow would convince her, but as a result of her refusal, she suffered declining health then sudden death.

Dad also hates doctors. He refuses to see a doctor no matter how sick he is. He thinks doctors kill more people than healing them, "burying their mistakes," something I witnessed too often throughout my training and subsequent years in nursing. Another reason for Dad despising doctors, his mother died in a hospital, and Dad, of course, blamed the hospital. Yet, he never seemed upset that I had chosen a hospital for my basic training.

Most of all, my father absolutely hated my grandmother he knew only as a very possessive woman, and he was certain she had ruined his marriage with my mother. He also understood that my grandmother had done everything she could to poison my mind against him and made me afraid to see him when he suddenly re-appeared in my life after seven years.

My father went through a period of extreme grief when my mother died he loved her so deeply. He was also deeply hurt by my not wanting anything to do with him until he contacted me at County. My grandmother had me believing my father had deserted me until I found out from him he had left because he could see a nasty custody battle was brewing with my grandmother and he didn't want to put me through that mess. Yet Dad such an eccentric and so thoroughly committed to his work, I'm sure he would have been hard to live with. So in a peculiar way, living with my grandmother was for me the lesser of two evils since despite the fact that she could be abusive, she provided the stability I needed after Mother died.

Dad is very perceptive and honest with me about my self-defeating problems and attitudes. Dad also warned me about Rick, my very possessive Latino boyfriend, even when I didn't want to face the truth. If Dad also thinks that I am wrong about something or someone, he will tell me calmly that he disagrees with me and why. And I find he is usually right.

Reading reviews of Dad's plays reveals that his work had been well received and predicted a successful career as an "up and coming" playwright. Yet he apparently had limited success due to his adamant insistence that no one change a single word of what he had written, his resistance so unyielding and so strong he eventually lost his only remaining contract with RKO and was blacklisted among all the other Hollywood studios for which he had once worked.

As a result, Dad had never fully succeeded after his one claimed success for the screenplay of a highly popular film at the time for which he received residuals on which along with promotional jobs he had survived the rest of his life, the residuals passed onto his daughter and then his grandchildren. Yet for all the acclaim of that singular success, from the scant information on that film, he apparently had shared credit for the screenplay with someone else, other reviews of the film crediting him with only the story, just as his highly acclaimed stage play produced on Broadway had been written by two leading playwrights of the period Ben Hecht and Charles McArthur using the storyline Dad had developed with writing partner Harriet, that play staged for a year under the title *Swan Song*. How much credit or reward Dad and Harriet had earned for that storyline is also unavailable, other than the repeated references of the play in reviews of his other plays produced and staged in local community playhouses. Reading through the several scripts he left behind, the storylines of the plays appear either dated or had been done with great success by others and that he had written more than one play on the subject of the Great Emancipator's spouse (*Mrs. Lincoln*) designed to fit the style and repeated success of a specific actress. Thus, while these plays had received favorable and even laudatory reviews, none had been produced as film and some only staged as plays at the Pasadena Playhouse. Finally, Dad at the time of his death had several unpublished novels, but those two were for some reason lost after I had tried finding a publisher without any success.

Ricardo Rojas, my "boyfriend" while I am in training at County was born in East Los Angeles of first generation Latino parents from Nicaragua. Twenty-four years young with blue eyes, black hair cut short, of medium height and optimum weight for his height, his coloring about like mine, he was as handsome as his brother Juan. His style of dress always casual consisting of jeans and t-shirt always worn beneath a blue suede jacket, "Rick" to those who knew him well was always polite and very cordial to me the whole time I knew him.

Yet I learned soon enough that he was very possessive and as a result other men were afraid of him. I never thought of him as a tough guy or gangbanger, but apparently he was. As time went on, Rick didn't want me to have any friends. He said he was jealous of my dad, even jealous of the time I spent studying for any of my classes. When he took me with him to see his friends, I noticed they didn't look at me and would never speak to me directly.

We students used to go across the street from the hospital to a taco stand where the tacos were tasty and inexpensive. The owner was Mexican, and we always had fun joking with him. Then one time I went to the taco stand with Rick, and the taco man would not look at me or speak to me. I saw the taco man later when I wasn't with Rick and asked him why he had acted so distant when before he had been so friendly.

He told me as a matter of fact, "I don't want to get knifed."

Surprised by his remark, I said, "Rick wouldn't hurt anybody!"

The taco man replied with some heat, "Miss, you don't know Latinos! After this, please buy your tacos at the stand down the street!"

Yet despite his reputation, Rick was honest, honorable, hard working, good to his parents, and he wanted to get his Associate Degree from East Los Angeles College where I met him in an introductory philosophy class while continuing work for a degree at UCLA I had attended before going into training at County.

Rick definitely liked girls, and he, as apparently so many other Latinos, viewed women as tokens of their masculine status. Rick generally seemed very calm, cool, and controlled when we were alone, told me many times that I was perfect for him, but he would grow upset if I talked about other friends. So he was very possessive. Then I learned that women in Latino culture thought when a man was possessive, his attitude meant he loved you and wanted to protect you.

One time when I was on OB, I asked a Mexican mother of ten children what to do about Rick. She surprised me by exclaiming:

"You are so lucky to have him! You should marry him quickly before someone else gets him! All you really need in life is a man who protects you, loves children, and you both have the blessing of the Virgin Mother who gives you many chamacos!"

She seemed so happy, but I knew if I who so loved my freedom followed her advice, I would have been so miserable. Yet what the woman told me was the first time I understood that each culture has a different view of life and love.

Rick loved to ride his motorcycle, but he took a lot of chances when at that time riders didn't wear helmets or protective clothing. To the total shock of my classmates, I once rode at top speed with Rick right through the L.A. freeway interchange. I have never been so scared!

Rick sometimes had a beer, but he didn't smoke, something I was thankful for, since my dad smoked continuously, as did my aunts, and I was always repulsed by filled ashtrays and second-hand smoke.

Similar to many Latinos, Rick would live with his parents and brother until or even after he married. His parents born in Nicaragua spoke hesitant English with a heavy accent. Rick worked in construction as laborer to help them with his support. Rick had one brother also very handsome. Rick and I used to double date with Zan and Juan, but Zan finally quit seeing Juan because she thought he was so boring, and he, too, was becoming possessive.

On one occasion Rick took me to the Yamashiro Restaurant tea room high on top one of the Hollywood Hills over looking the city. After all these years, I still recall that date, the last one we had but not the last time I saw Rick. He must have been considering doing that for some time given his usual attire of t-shirt, jeans, and blue suede jacket and that we always used his motorcycle when we weren't double dating with Zan and Juan.

Rick surprised me by informing me when bringing me back to the hospital after an outing on his motorcycle that he wanted to take me some place special and he would like me to dress for the occasion. Of course, the only thing I had that might fit the occasion was the blue dress I always wore to work at the May Company Wilshire, but since I had nothing fancier, I decided that would have to suffice.

When Rick came for me at the hospital on the day of the special event, he surprised me by arriving alone in his brother Juan's car, Rick wearing a suit, white shirt and tie, and polished shoes as if he were going to church for some special sacrament. He climbed out to cordially greet me and came around to hold open the door while I entered, our performance witnessed by Zan and Linda and all the others lounging on the barrack balcony gawking at us. I embarrassed, waved at them and turn away as Rick climbed in behind the wheel and took us away, but I had no idea as to where we might be going, and Rick offered no clue.

We reached Hollywood and climbed along a route I had often driven with Uncle Ned in his imported MG with right-hand steering wheel. As we climbed, I searched for Dad's house, thought I recognized it, and imagined him there with his dogs pounding away with two fingers on his typewriter in his basement room off the patio. Way off in the distance, on this surprisingly clear day without smog, the white, massive bulk of County rose above the plain of East L.A.

I gazed in wonder when we arrived at the Yamashiro Restaurant with its tea room I had heard of so often located on its own hill hundreds of feet above Hollywood Blvd. From my wide reading of Hollywood lore when I was still a child, I had learned that "Yamashiro" means "Mountain Palace" applied to the mansion built between 1911 and 1914 by two wealthy brothers to house their priceless collection of Asian art and treasures using craftsman brought especially from Asia to replicate a palace in the Yamashiro province of Japan. Before the Great Depression and World War Two, the original mansion had been surrounded by terracing with 30,000 varieties of plants and trees as well as waterfalls, ponds with gold fish, a private zoo of exotic birds and monkeys, a lake with rare black Australian swans, all at a cost of what now would be 50 million US dollars. Anti-Japanese prejudice during the 1940's resulted in much of the original structures being either destroyed by fire or damaged by vandals or by attempts to disguise the Asian features until refurbished after the war into the present restaurant.

Greeted by a hostess in traditional geisha gown and manner, we were led to a table on a terrace overlooking Hollywood where we settled and where I used the rare clear view to avoid looking at Rick and meeting Ricks' study of my response.

I searched again for Dad's house that should be visible in the area but I couldn't locate it, most likely because of Rick's steady inspection, and I soon became uncomfortable and I knew I needed to respond to his close inspection.

"This is elegant," I offered.

"It's perfect," he replied, "Just like you."

I smiled in response. "You always say that. This is way more elegant than me. The prices seem a bit much. Can you really afford it?"

"You're worth every penny," he replied just as we were served a casual tea certainly different than Mexican, making me wonder again why we were here.

"What's the occasion?" I asked and looked out at the Hollywood scene below bracing myself for Rick's reply.

A day or two or three later, I fond time to meet Dad to tell him about Rick and our date at the tea house that clearly indicated Rick becoming ever more possessive.

"Dad, he wants us to get married!"

"Do you love him?"

"I like him a lot. But marry him?"

"There's a big world out there, Ramona!" Dad advises. "If you don't love him and aren't willing to commit yourself to him for the rest of your days, get him out of your life! He will just keep trying to possess you, isolate you, smother you just like your grandmother did!"

I have no ready answer and silently study his stern expression, and as always, I know he is right.

When I talked to Zan later and told her of the incident at the tea house and of Dad's advice, she also thought Rick far too interested in me, someone who wanted to own me, so she totally agreed with Dad and disapproved of my even considering accepting Rick's proposal, warning me of the danger that lay ahead if I didn't find some way out of what she suspected had become a "full blown" affair.

"Besides, if, as I suspect from what you've implied you've been doing more than just going out on dates, I'm surprised he wants to marry you since you're no longer pure."

"He says he loves me!" I replied, upset by her voicing what I knew as true. "He still insists I'm perfect for him!"

"For how long until he finds someone fresh? How many chamacos are you willing to carry for him?"

I recalled my conversation with the Mexican mother of ten. I recalled my response to what the woman advised, my having remained silent, then moving off onto the ward filled with other women who had recently delivered yet another soul into the light.

But how could I ease out of such a situation when doing so might be as difficult as finally freeing myself from Babu? I didn't want to hurt Rick since I did care for him. I certainly didn't want to anger him since learning of his reputation as someone who must be treated with respect.

So after my anxious stewing over what might be the best path for me to follow, with graduation from training drawing near that would launch me into the frightening world at large, I pondered my options once I left County while at the same time I reviewed what I had learned from others and what I had learned about myself over the previous three years.

We were Probies from September until December 1954 when we became student nurses until June, 1955, moved to the two-story barracks referred to as cottages, and became Juniors until June, 1956, when we became Seniors until we graduated in June, 1957. I along with my other classmates after having sat for and having passed the State Boards for my RN certificate, I receive at the graduation ceremony the coveted black velvet band to be placed across the brim of my cap.

During the ceremony I look out at the crowd and see my dad smiling and looking handsome in his dark suit sitting next to a woman I think I recognize as Harriet, his writing partner. After the ceremony, I exchange congratulations with Zan and Linda who leave, Zan with her mother and father, aunt and uncle, Linda with a current boyfriend, and I move to greet Dad remembering what happened at my capping almost three years ago, not knowing what to expect this time and, as usual, I am somewhat anxious.

I thank Dad for attending my graduation ceremony.

He gives me a hug and his smoochy kiss.

"Ramona, you remember Harriet."

I acknowledge that I do and tell her that I am glad to see her again and that she had come with Dad to see me graduate. She smiles, offers me a big hug, and congratulates me on receiving my diploma.

"So nice to see you again, Ramona. How many years has it been since we last saw each other?"

"It has been a while. Long before Mother became so sick. How have you been?"

"I'm doing OK considering that I always have to deal with your father!"

Dad and Harriet both laugh.

"You certainly have changed!" Harriet offers. "All grown up! So beautiful. You should be in films like your lovely mother. But now you're a nurse. My that is a change. How'd that happen?"

"A long story I'd prefer not to tell just now. Maybe once everything sinks in and I feel settled."

Dad apparently sees where all this might be going and redirects the conversation. "Well, Ramona, where would you like to celebrate? Since we have Harriet's car, we could go anywhere you'd like."

"Or we could try out usual place unless you want to try someplace different."

"Well, we know the foods good and the price is something we can afford."

At the Mexican restaurant, once we have settled and ordered, Dad asks me, "Ramona, I guess I wasn't paying attention, but it seems I didn't hear your name called when they were handing out the diplomas."

"Well, they clearly called my name, and I got my diploma after three years of hard labor!"

"Can it see it?"

"Not much to see. It's just like every other diploma."

"I'd just like to see it. Do you mind?"

"No, of course not."

I hand him to diploma. He opens the cover.

"Joan Grey!" Who's Joan Grey!"

"Your daughter." I offer quietly.

He studies me, his dark, gypsy eyes questioning.

"I decided I wanted a different name when I enrolled in County."

He waits, continuing his study.

"I didn't know where you were." I begin. "When I didn't hear a word from you in years, I thought just as Babu always claimed that you had deserted me and didn't really care if I existed. So I decided that Ramona Romero had died with my mother and I decided to assume Mother's name as mine along with the name of someone whom I considered at the time my patron saint."

"Why haven't you told me before! I've been calling you Ramona all this time! Why didn't you tell me! People in Hollywood are always changing their names!"

Although my dad acts matter-of-fact about my name change and tries to appear as if he is indifferent, I can sense that he is hurt.

Harriet, as always, comes to the rescue. "So what are you going to do now that you've finished training? Stay on at County?"

"I might. But I'd really like to finish the degree I started at UCLA."

Dad still isn't saying anything when we receive our food and we begin to eat.

"I've always loved literature and philosophy," I say to Harriet. "Both have helped me, especially literature that allows me to escape to other places and other people's lives and leave mine behind. I probably got that from my dad."

Dad sits back from his plate. "Well, escape sometimes does help deal with the world of hard knocks." Then he studies me again. "You've always had a rich imagination, Ramona!" Then he stops, looks pained, and grins his gypsy grin. "I guess I won't ever stop calling you Ramona. Your new name sounds so cold."

"Daddy, you can call me whatever you like,"

"As long as it's in good taste!" Harriet adds.

We all laugh breaking the tense mood and return to our food.

How nice to be sharing this event pleasantly with understanding, so unlike what we experienced here in this same setting after my capping almost three years ago. So I begin to anticipate what I might experience in the days ahead.

Having decided on the next big move in my life, I've been dreading this day when I have to tell Dad I'm leaving L.A., something I haven't even hinted at before, and I know telling him will be hard because I am certain of his response.

We're sitting on his patio. The piano player is at it again, the now familiar melodies we've heard over and over again rising to us on warm, smog-thick air from below. Dad is reading one of the three papers he routinely reads that report the latest Hollywood scandals and film studio productions. I listen to the distant piano player endlessly practicing what I know are preludes and studies from when I had practiced them myself. I had been good at them once, everyone loudly praising my accomplishment until I abandoned playing them like most everything else I had abandoned after Mother's death.

"Dad?" I begin with trepidation. "I don't know any easy way to tell you. I'm thinking of leaving L.A."

"What!" Dad looks up stunned. He drops his paper. "Where you going?"

"The Bay Area. San Francisco."

"San Francisco? For how long?"

"I don't know, Dad. I'm thinking about transferring from UCLA to UC Berkeley to study philosophy and literature. I've heard Cal is a great school, the best public university in the world and the only one I can afford. But for now, I just need to leave. I can't stay in L.A. any longer."

My dad looks hurt – almost bitter – as if life is dealing him yet another blow, one of those hard knocks he is always warning me about. "You can't stay? Why are you going, Ramona, when we're finally getting to know each other again?"

"Everything's changing for me, Dad. Nursing has changed for me. The idealism I once had of helping people and saving lives and making the world a better place is gone. L.A. has changed, all this smog and heat, so many people too often fighting each other, and no one reaching out to help each other. What I see now is no longer the City of Angels I grew up in. Most of all, I've changed. I'm not the same person I was. Training to be a nurse changes people. In some ways I feel a better person but nursing also has made me somewhat cynical and hard and sometimes bitter. You know a while back I almost burned out completely. I'm better now. Things seem a bit clearer, cleaner, brighter. I'll miss you Dad, I really will. But leaving this place is something I have to do. I have to leave Hollywood, the dream factory, forever behind. "Dream factory!" Isn't that what everyone calls it? Well, now my dream is different. I have to follow a different path and try to fulfill my new dream."

Dad studies me, searches my face, searches the smog-bound hills that descend from where we sit in heat and hazy sunshine. We listen to the piano player beginning again the piece we have heard so often. Dad takes a deep breath. We remain silent for a long spell. Dad finally with a sigh begins.

"In a way I know how you feel, Ramona. I left my family in Florida and everyone I knew to go to New York City. I was barely 17 and I knew absolutely nothing about life. I had no money, no place to live. I was lucky. A Jewish family took me in off the street. Why, I will never know. But they must have seen something in me that they thought worthy of their support, and I finally got a job on a local paper and learned enough to eventually become a reporter. I felt sad because of my mother. She was terribly hurt when I left Florida. She couldn't understand why I had to leave. But I wanted to become a part of show business, so I couldn't stay in Florida. I had to go to New York! I had to at least try to make it on Broadway! I dreamed about becoming a playwright, and to some extent I've succeeded, although not as much I've wanted. Does anyone ever reach their goal? 'Oh, that our reach should exceed our grasp!' So I understand your feelings, Ramona. I'm sorry you're leaving, especially when we seem to be resolving most of our issues, but I do understand why you have to leave as something you just have to do just as I did."

Dad rises, comes to me, holds out his hand. I reach to grab it. He pulls me up into his arms and his embrace. The piano player down the hill finishes in a flourishing crescendo.

I feel better now with a big weight lifted off me. Time now to go back to the hospital, start to pack, gather myself to say goodbye to Zan and Linda who are also getting ready to leave, Zan who most likely will return to Salem, Oregon, Linda to wherever she might wander seeking some place to settle and perhaps find peace. Our class that has grown so close we were almost like a family I never had but one that is slowly but surely beginning to dissolve. Dad offers me a ride and surprises me further when instead of dropping me off at the nearest bus stop, we move on by without slowing, heading for the Macy Street bridge crossing to East L.A. and the Los Angeles County General Hospital that rises above us in all its massive, shining glory.

A week later, Dad surprises me again by coming all the way to County to take me and my luggage to the bus station in downtown Los Angeles.

We try to get an early start while the temperature is still cool, but L.A. has already begun another day of oppressive heat and stifling smog. When Dad comes to get me at the hospital, he has been up all night working on a new project, and he appears more weary and rumpled than ever. I guess he isn't afraid to come into this dangerous neighborhood during the day, not like the time when he refused because he once was attacked by Zootsuiters when he was driving cab at night.

As we drive away, I gaze back at the soaring monumental edifice where I have spent the previous three years of my life, the structure becoming smaller but still majestic as I turn and face forward pondering what might be ahead.

The Greyhound bus station is crowded with a lot of weird but typical people waiting for or changing buses. I buy my ticket and Dad and I wait on a bench for my bus to leave. I feel a mingling of excitement and sadness. I will miss my friends, even the hospital, but most of all I'll miss my dad. I can tell he feels very sad that I'm leaving.

"Call me as soon as you get to San Francisco."

I nod. "I will, Dad."

"Where will you be staying? The Y? You better. It's safer. You most likely will start looking for work right away."

"I have to."

"You need money?"

"Dad, I always need money!"

"Here, Ramona, take this." Dad hands me a twenty dollar bill, a major gift for him.

"Thanks, Dad, that will help a lot!"

I have managed somehow to save a couple of hundred dollars that won't last long, so I know I'd better find work right away, but I also know I will because after my training at County and what I've seen of life: birth, death, all those sick and suffering patients, and even though I won't be 21 until November, I know with confidence I'm well-prepared.

We sit in stifling heat among the multitude and wait in silence. Then I hear the call:

"Coach 807 departing for Santa Barbara, Santa Maria, Salinas, San Jose, San Francisco! All aboard!"

I suddenly feel like crying. I have a sudden rush of fear and doubt. I think of my ride with Aunt Jessie to Los Angeles County General Hospital to start training. How long ago that now seems.

Dad puts his hand on my shoulder. He looks anxious, maybe because he is losing me again, although he would never admit it.

"When will I hear from you, Ramona?"

"As soon as I get a job, Dad, and I find a place to live."

"You sure you're going to be all right? You don't know one soul in the Bay Area!"

"I'll be fine, Dad. Don't worry. Nothing could be worse than Los Angeles County General Hospital."

The driver slams and latches the luggage doors, climbs up onto his seat, starts the engine sending up clouds of exhaust to join the smog, the diesel rattling and roaring.

Time for me to say goodbye. Dad hugs me and gives me one of his mushy kisses. My turn to climb up into the bus where I find a seat next to a window.

There's my dad waiting for the bus to leave. I can't tell how Dad is feeling right now. He might be a little bitter that I'm leaving just when we were getting to know each other again. The bus door closes and we start moving out of the station. I wave at Dad; he waves back.

As my bus pulls out onto the street, I leave Dad behind standing alone on the curb looking around him as if he were abandoned or lost, wondering what to do or where to go next. Then as we move through long familiar streets toward Highway 101, I think I see, or imagine I see, a young man with blue eyes, black hair cut short, t-shirt, jeans and blue suede jacket raise his hand in a final farewell.

Three Unlikely Companions

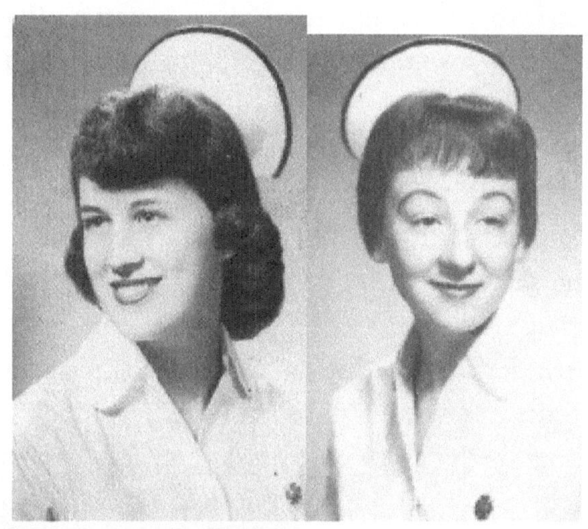

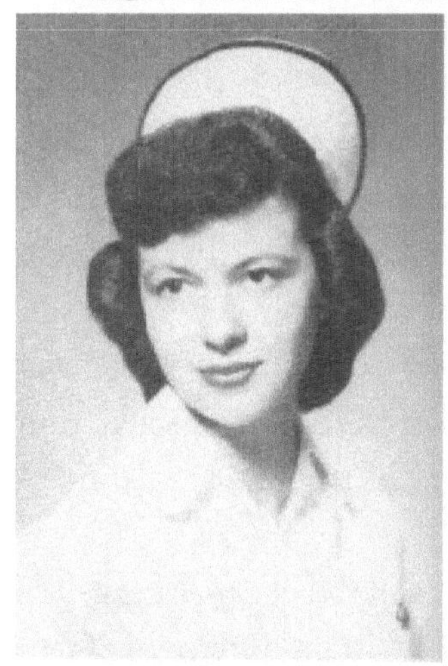

Zan from Salem, Oregon; Linda from Des Moines, Iowa (by way of Van Nuys, California; and I, Joan (aka Ramona) from Los Angles, California couldn't be more unlike each other except we were all 18 when we started training. Yet despite or perhaps because of our differences we grew to become best friends since we were always together as much as our training would allow. Zan the quiet, sensible one; Linda often wild and cynical; I somewhere between, usually sensible, mostly due to my always being afraid I would do something wrong that would lead to failure and rejection, I sometimes had a somber side that could turn my mind very dark. So I also had an inner life that could be good or bad, my ability to live a second or even third life saving me when I thought I couldn't stand another minute of training or living in the actual world.

Our differences also were displayed in our appearance: The three of us were about the same ethnicity – although I did have Jewish, Romanian gypsy heritage from Dad's side of our family. Zan with blue eyes, Linda with green, I with dark brown, our eyes complementing our hair color and style: Zan with dark brown page boy, Linda with red hair and pixie bangs, I with black page boy or ponytail. Zan and I were about the same height of five and a half feet, Linda short, small, a naughty elf who just wanted to have a good time and rarely serious about anything but often cynical about life, although she didn't display her cynicism to patients who always enjoyed her spontaneous antics.

Zan compared to Linda sometimes seemed somewhat dull. While Zan and I had occasional disagreements, we never had a real argument. Zan a very pleasant, supportive friend was always there for me. For example, the time my dad suddenly appeared out of nowhere arriving unannounced at the entrance to the hospital after years of separation and I didn't want to see him because Babu had so brainwashed me, I actually was afraid to meet him.

According to Babu, my dad was a selfish and evil person caring only about himself and his work. In a way her accusations were valid except that Dad was not evil; he was actually a good person if you could see under that thick cloak of bitterness and cynicism he wrapped around himself.

In any case, I didn't want to meet with him. When I heard that he was waiting in the lobby of the hospital. I wasn't going to go, but Zan – bless her – said that she would go with me, so crossing my arms tightly, I walked with Zan to the Acute Unit lobby entrance where I saw my dad looking every bit as anxious as I felt, probably afraid that I would refuse to meet or talk with him, a very awkward moment, all three of us standing in silence. I finally gave Dad a hug and he gave me one of his smoochy kisses, and I said:

"Hello, Dad. Where have you been all of these years?"

He told me he would explain and that we should sit down on one of the nearby benches. Zan said goodbye, smiled at my dad, and left.

If it hadn't been for Zan, I probably never would have gone to meet my dad, and I would have left him standing in the lobby waiting until he got tired and had finally left the hospital angry.

Zan also offered her support in our Senior year when she warned me that Linda and I were taking some very risky chances sneaking out late at night with truck drivers who delivered supplies to the hospital, riding with them in their big rigs to a near-by drive-in where they would buy us coffee and anything else we wanted, a very welcomed offer since we didn't have enough money to buy really good food for ourselves and hospital cafeteria food almost inedible. Then they would take us back to the hospital, we'd say good-bye to our truck driver and sneak back into the dorm, lay down for a few hours of sleep, then get up and go on duty. Sometimes we drove around all night with them while they made deliveries and when we finally got back to our barracks at around 5:00 a.m., we would hop into the shower, throw on our uniforms, and go on duty with no sleep at all. This practice was especially bad if we had to double back for duty the same night so we often had very little sleep for almost 24 hours. I hope we didn't kill any patients because we were so tired we could easily have done something wrong, maybe serious, leading to what we claimed about burying our mistakes.

Zan insisted I stop running around at night because I surely would eventually get caught and expelled. I did quit but Linda kept right on going out with truckers. Zan also said that we were very lucky that these men were so nice to us and didn't try to touch us or demand some favor in exchange for what they bought us. But I did find out later that one of the truckers was in love with me, and one night I woke up blinded by a flashlight. Linda's then current boyfriend, later said I didn't scream or anything and that I was so cool. He lay down next to me and we talked for a short while until I told him to leave. If a housemother had found out that a man was in my room at night, I definitely would have been expelled. I told Zan what had happened, but not Linda since the man supposedly was Linda's boyfriend and she would have been upset, and that little redhead could really get mad and cause trouble. Zan told me that episode was very scary and I was lucky that Linda's boyfriend was such a nice guy but the situation could have been really nasty. Another guy who wasn't so nice could have tried to rape me or kill me and that I had better quit going with truckers. If Linda wanted to take such dumb chances so be it, but Zan knew I was simply going along with Linda for the ride. So even if I was actually somewhat reserved, I did have a wild side, and one of my patients once said that what I really wanted was to ride the rails as he had and leave County and nursing school because they were too tame. Yet I wasn't stupid and I knew I would have hated being kicked out at that late stage in training when I was a Senior and just about to graduate.

Linda with her typical abandon always brought some much needed comedy into our lives. The three of us had a good time together. Linda was closer to me than to Zan, but then, I wasn't as conservative as Zan. Linda and I also had experienced childhoods that were not anywhere as stable as Zan's. Linda had an unhappy childhood and hated her parents, while I had an unusual and strange childhood with both my parents in show business, and I had also lost my mother when I was still very young.

During our three years in training, we believed our greatest achievement would be to graduate from County and earn our RN. Zan and I thought getting good grades and being highly thought of by our instructors and well-regarded by our patients very important. Linda, however, didn't care much about her grades as long as she passed, and she didn't really care about the judgment of our instructors as long as they didn't kick her out of school. Linda thought being liked by her patients and keeping them comfortable and amused most important. Zan was an excellent student, and a good nurse, while Linda was bright enough but took little interest in her studies.

Unlike Linda, Zan had a good attitude toward life, and she dealt well with problems. But, in all honesty, I now perceive Zan as a bit of a prude and a "goody–goody" kind of person. Never breaking any rules, Zan was a "straight arrow." Linda, whom we often called a little devil dared do anything, even if dangerous. She felt strongly that the best way to get through life was to take an "I don't give a damn attitude," an attitude that eventually led to bad results.

Zan and I were quite good at book-learning. I, however, was terrible at performing mechanical tasks, one of the biggest requirements in nursing. I wonder now how I got through training, received my RN once I graduated, and practiced my profession successfully for years. I fortunately was able to absorb and put my book-learning to work in practical situations so I survived training even though learning some nursing skills was really hard. I don't think Linda was terribly book-smart, but she was able to put what she learned to good use.

Zan was a supportive friend, and she helped me get through some difficult situations. Linda's main virtue was her sense of humor and that she rarely acted sad, although I think that she actually was very unhappy and used her flippant attitude to keep from collapsing under the weight of her anger at her parents and her cynicism and outrage at life in general. Most of the time, I laughed at her antics, and Linda also could be supportive and help me look at problems from a different perspective than Zan's.

We all loved Mexican food that we could afford on our monthly pay of $30 from County and whatever we earned extra as aides, a taco stand conveniently across the street from the hospital and the food at the hospital always seemingly so gross it could—as we used to say—"gag a maggot."

Since we never had any money for entertainment, sometimes we would attend an interesting court case almost as good as a movie but a lot cheaper.

While we were in training, none of us smoked, drank, or took illegal drugs. However, we occasionally did take Benzedrine to stay awake when studying for a test, but I think that the "bennies from heaven" didn't actually help much. Ideas that seemed terrific when we were on them at night seemed really stupid the next morning, so being on bennies was a real mind-trip that went nowhere. We also took Ritalin from medical ward supply shelves. Ritalin didn't suppress appetite, which was good since I didn't need to get any thinner (Linda always called me "Boney Joanie") but helped with cognition, made me feel more alert, and didn't cause the irrational thoughts caused by bennies. When we left the hospital on weekends or vacations, our bags were checked by our ever vigilant housemothers searching for drugs as if we were so stupid we would hide drugs in our bags.

Zan had a good relationship with her parents. I never heard her complain about her childhood. I visited Zan's parents in Salem, Oregon on one vacation, and I recall that they were very pleasant and welcoming. Linda hated her parents and was happy to get away from Des Moines. I an only child had a complicated relationship with my parents. I never heard Linda or Zan discuss any siblings. Zan's father and mother were alive while we were in training, but I knew nothing about Linda's parents except that she hated them. Linda had a troubled childhood and had no use for her parents, and she came into training partially to get away from home, the same as I did to get away from Babu.

As for most students, our financial situation was dire. Earning only a dollar a day, from that largess, we had to pay for uniforms and books and fees. I was fortunate because I had a scholarship for my first year as a Probie, and I also got my books and uniforms free. But I still had a big money problem. Babu had cut off all financial support, and once I graduated from high school, she demanded I pay for board and room. So I received no financial help from her or from my dad. Thirty dollars didn't take us very far, allowing us an occasional taco at an East L.A. taco stand where we had to avoid gangs, or we might see a movie at a cut-rate movie theatre once every six months, or purchase a few inexpensive trinkets to keep up our spirits.

As we only received $30.00 a month from County, Linda and I worked most of our days off as aides at other hospitals, a practice that was prohibited in 1959 with the adoption of a revised curriculum.[17] When Linda and I decided to get jobs in other hospitals, we worked at Kaiser and Cedars of Lebanon or Good Samaritan because these hospitals needed a constant supply of extra help always poorly paid. We were able to make beds, give baths, and feed patients, and we were fast and efficient and the patients loved us. We were young, enthusiastic, and caring, all the precious motives the old graduates had lost long ago.

During summer vacations, Zan would go home to be with her parents. Linda and I didn't have anywhere we really wanted to go on our breaks from training, so we worked. The summer between our Junior and Senior year, Linda and I rented a small apartment across from Cedars of Lebanon and worked nights as aides. Linda got to work on the "Movie Star" floor, and I was assigned to care for the patients who were only wealthy.

Dad would often bring us lunch from a local delicatessen. Dad thought Linda cute, and she thought him a real "trip." Linda also had a current boy friend who visited us occasionally. I didn't trust him, and I found having him around difficult, especially when I was off duty and Linda was working. Yet, Linda and I had interesting vacations and earned extra money to supplement our meager pay while in training.

Working in these other hospitals made us understand what a great hospital County was despite all its problems and that the care our patients received at County was as good in many ways as the care patients received in private hospitals. Of course, the patients at County with strange, unusual, and horrible diseases were likely to receive the most attention from the doctors and consequently from us as we carried out all of the doctor's orders. Sad to say, if you were just a run-of-the-mill patient with pneumonia, or cancer (unless rare), or cirrhosis of the liver from too much cheap booze, you were pretty much ignored by the doctors but not by us.

The profession of nursing too often was looked down on during the time I was in training. As Babu said, nurses were just the slaves of physicians, commanded to rise when a doctor entered the room or follow him into an elevator then stand aside to allow him to leave, and always expected to follow the doctor's orders even when we knew he was clearly wrong. Yet, if we knew that he had ordered the wrong drug for a patient or a dangerous drug, we were supposed to refuse to give the drug and even grab it out of his hand if he tried to give the drug himself, so we were supposed to be obedient but also aggressive when necessary.

Note that I always say "he" when referring to doctors since there were very few women doctors at the time, and nursing was a woman's occupation, with most people really not thinking of nursing as a true profession the same as medicine or law. Babu, although a trained nurse herself, always spoke with scorn about nurses and would always demand,

"Why don't you become a doctor or a lawyer! Why a nurse? If you're a nurse, you're powerless! No one respects you! Doctors are gods! Nurses are slaves for scrubbing floors, washing dishes, cleaning instruments, taking care of patients no matter how difficult, while doctors receive all the glory! Make something of yourself! Don't be a nurse!"

Yet, at County we were offered the best training available. The 1650 bed hospital provided 4,000 to 6,000 patients yearly for us to learn and diagnosis every disease or health problem that afflicts humankind. But because of low pay and high demands on energy and health, with always a shortage of RNs, County always was very poorly staffed, so we students pretty much ran the hospital. [18]

We often were told almost as a mantra that if you stayed at County long enough, you'd eventually see every disease both mental and physical that needed treatment. As a result of what we experienced, we students all believed that once we graduated from training at County we could work anywhere because so much had been expected of us, too often without the necessary instruction and experience, and we emerged from training very confident that no matter what our level of training, we would never be unemployed.

The gravest sin during training and grounds for expulsion: a student openly complaining to instructors or head nurses about working under such demanding conditions or expressing the slightest fear of not being able to perform a procedure, or take care of a critically ill patient, or run a ward at night with only the help of an aide and an orderly, the only truly experienced staff who were actually running the ward and really knew how many mistakes we made and how many of our poor patients we buried because we didn't really know what we were doing and how to do it.

Our main move was "to play the role" and act with confidence that we knew what we were doing. If you played the role well enough, you would look like a nurse, seemed to act like a nurse, and you were OK. Only the patients weren't always OK. But since most patients had been treated worse in life, they lived in spite of our inept skills and ignorance or were buried because of our mistakes.

Linda's rebellious attitude didn't seem to bother Miss Loftus, having dealt with other rebellious teenagers who usually calmed down and reformed in the end to avoid expulsion. In my case, I was inwardly rebellious and defiant and I tried not to show it just as I had done with my grandmother. But I could only hide the depth of my feelings for so long, and they finally came out, especially the anger and hate I felt towards people who had a captive audience and wanted to control other people.

In the end, I wasn't enslaved by their dominance forever. I got away from Babu by going into training and got away from Miss Loftus by graduating from County. In both cases, my goal was to become free to live my life the way I wanted without anyone trying to control my every thought and action. So I won out over Miss Loftus just as I had won over Babu, eventually escaping them both once I had the opportunity through training and education. Of course, I soon met other people after I graduated who were so much like them, but those others didn't bother me. I knew how to handle them by staying away from such people and if I had to be with them not let them get close by keeping my distance and never allowing them to enter my inner circle of thoughts and feelings and dreams of success.

None of us belonged to a church, although we claimed belief in Christianity. None of us knew much about love. We were just too young to feel such a deep emotion, Of course, we all had male friends with whom we went on dates.

When I was sixteen, I had gone out with a war veteran who seemed very sophisticated because he had been through a lot in Korea as a non-commissioned officer in a reconnaissance platoon and he told me about how he had watched his best friends die. He was also well-educated and the son of a prominent judge who had become wealthy. But Jack was 25, so Babu decided he was too old for me and she drove him off, even though I liked him a lot, and he never was anything but nice to me. When we were going out together, we did not have a romantic or intimate relationship, only a friendship, although I knew he wanted more. During the time we were together I had a spell of mild depression, anxiety, and disorientation (aka, a nervous breakdown) caused by my unresolved grief over Mother's death. I still cried a lot over my loss, and Babu didn't help by ending my friendship with Jack. His being an adult, she was afraid he was going to take advantage of me and that I would have been a willing victim. [In an email, Paula Strahm offered the following: "Jack was a very good looking man, very smart, a grad of USC, son of a judge, and he lived next door to me. One thing I felt he required in any woman worthy of his interest was intelligence which Joan definitely had. Before dating Joan, Jack dated my sister, who is also extremely intelligent. When my sister went away to college, Jack took quite an interest in Joan, and Babu was wise to keep them apart because she was way too young."]

I am almost certain Linda was having sex with various so-called boyfriends who were always older. She was "fast" and a real "chick" as they said in those days. I'm surprised she didn't get pregnant while we were in training. Zan, in contrast was viewed as somewhat innocent as she wasn't really involved with anyone during training. I had a Latino boyfriend who was horribly possessive, one reason why I decided to leave for San Francisco to break free from the "full-blown" affair that had developed. But we thankfully were all heterosexual. Had we offered even a suggestion of a different orientation at the time, Miss Loftus would have made sure we would have been expelled from training for what she considered a terrible illness if she ever had caught even a whiff of what in her eyes was worse than being a psychopath with a long rap sheet of sadistic murders.

Zan didn't have a boyfriend while we were in training, although she brief went out on double dates with my latino boyfriend and his brother, and she never mentioned that she had a boyfriend in high school. Linda had several boyfriends throughout our three years together, was definitely having sex with guys, and if she wasn't having sex, she was flirting and moving in that direction, with Zan a virgin, and I, as usual, somewhere between from my year-long affair with Rick. Linda could be really jealous, so I was really careful never to let her know that one of her boyfriends had broken into my room late one night, even though all we did was talk. Zan was never jealous but was somewhat protective of me as we were such close friends. I have never been a jealous or possessive person, so I am grateful I never had to endure the curse that could be so hurtful and even dangerous.

Zan was very well adjusted and was well-liked by everyone because she was such an honest and pleasant person. I think most of the other students enjoyed Linda because of her wild antics as well as her looking like a tiny red-headed imp. I believe I was generally well-liked by the other students both male and female.

One of my behaviors that either annoyed or amused other students was my constant griping about training and our poverty as students, about how badly I thought the patients were too often being treated, about my grandmother, about my dad. But I could be really funny at times. I was so totally L.A. and later East L.A. in my manner of speaking and moving by adopting the vocabulary and tone of voice of a gang member from East L.A. So I always had fun living a second or third life entirely different from my persona while in training or how I behaved when I was visiting my dad and his Hollywood friends and I acted as if I still wanted to be an actress or writer, which I did since I always felt that succeeding as a nurse was not nearly as satisfying if I had succeeded as a screenwriter or actor.

I most likely developed my attitude from my grandmother's contempt for nursing even though she was a nurse herself and both my dad and my mother had been successful in film production because they were talented and dedicated to their art. I would really have preferred to win a academy award than win an award for outstanding nursing care. I went into nursing because it was the wise thing to do at the time, and I did love learning about the human body, about medications and how they worked, about diseases and their treatment such as tuberculosis that had killed my mother. But I never liked floor nursing although I did find the patients endlessly interesting and so different from each other.

My attitude toward nursing probably showed, although I was never arrogant about my past life as Ramona Romero. I often wished my mother would have lived so I could have continued to work on my dream life which was connected with the arts. Nonetheless, I was popular with my classmates, and during my months as a Probie, I was elected by them as Miss Professional Standards. They also laughed at my need for smelling salts to stay awake in class because I rarely slept from being too busy seven days a week working as an aide to earn extra money and going to night school at East Los Angeles College where I met Rick in a philosophy class while tying to continue working toward getting my degree I had started at UCLA. The others laughed when they decided that I must have absorbed the information from my training classes via osmosis since I always made good grades and remembered everything that had been said by the teacher although I was half asleep.

In sum, I think we three had a good relationship with almost everyone, except Miss Loftus. I now find somewhat strange that all three of us got along as well as we did. I guess we balanced each other. In looking back on our years together, I'm not surprised that Zan became a devout Catholic with six kids and twenty grandkids, while Linda took full advantage of our friendship. She died of a drug overdose after living with me for a while in Daly City, a suburb of San Francisco, leaving a newborn son conceived with a drug dealer father.

During training we all had days when we felt that the worst mistake we ever made was going into training, especially at County. If only we could have chosen an easier profession such as secretarial work or teaching or being a librarian. We should have picked a profession that didn't break our backs and break our hearts every single day. Working and training and living at County was very difficult, the place always overheated, reeking from a stew of foul odors and we surrounded and overwhelmed by patients who were very sick, too often in great pain, often psychotic, or contagious, or dying, or stone cold dead, in which case we would have the unpleasant task of preparing them for the morgue.

No wonder we often joked about our jobs. Better to laugh than to cry. Even a private hospital for training perhaps would have been better, easier, and more gratifying. But then in the end most of us understood we had not made a mistake to have gone into training at County because we knew that we would have a profession and a job for life through the strength of character and self-confidence we had developed through our training.

Yet, many students did leave who couldn't cope and did feel that going into training was the worst mistake of their lives. When these students finally quit, we never knew what happened to them. Did they find happiness even if they discovered that nothing is easy in this world, and every job, every profession has problems? But for many, the toughest problems they ever faced were at County, and they left training within the first months before Capping when they pitched their dunce caps, ran out the entrance, down the stairs of the hospital, their mothers waiting for them in a car with engine running, their suitcases thrown into the trunk, they speeding away to some place less harsh, less frightening, less demanding. That they couldn't abide training held no shame. Not everyone was able to face the harsh life one faced at County. Not everyone could deal with all the pain, sickness, and death that we faced every single day. But those who stayed and survived gained a strength that helped them and others throughout their lives.

A life in retrospect

Ramona Romero (aka Joan Grey, a name she assumed upon entering training to become a nurse at Los Angeles County General Hospital School of Nursing), born November 6, 1935, Los Angles, CA, of Serbian heritage from her grandmother, Swedish from her mother, Romanian Jew from her father, with brown eyes, dark brown hair almost black usually in a pony tail, 5 ft. 4 inches and slender, skin tone always reminding Babu (her maternal grandmother) of Ramona's father and his Basque-Gypsy heritage.

Ramona was considered pretty when young, although she certainly didn't see herself that way, yet when still a child she had a screen test for a film role given to Natalie Wood, an equally beautiful woman similar in appearance because of Slavic heritage who had previous film experience.

Eighteen to just short of twenty-one during her years at Los Angeles County General Hospital School of Nursing, Ramona's mode of dress when not wearing a uniform was contemporary but very plain and causal, mostly skirts and sweaters, bobby socks and special shoes since she had bad feet always painful.

[20]

She often didn't know how she made it through nursing school with those feet. She also had an awkward walk often painful because of her bad feet. People in training sometimes commented on how she walked tipping from side to side, so she thought perhaps one leg must have been a little shorter than the other and she should have had special shoes that would have corrected the problem but never did because of the expense and because she accepted her painful walk as just another challenge she would always have to endure. Not receiving any medical care while in training except for physical therapy twice a week for a time to treat problems that were developing even during her early years, she would later wonder how she got through nursing school with the pain that she often had to endure.

During her first months of training as a probationer, Ramona to her chagrin was elected Miss Professional Standards, a duty she found odious having to stand at the entrance to the hospital school, the towering, massive white edifice at her back, as she inspected students including her friends for any faults in their appearance. She never understood why she was chosen for what to her was an embarrassing chore, especially when some classmates got even by whispering loud enough for her to hear that she apparently didn't take showers because they never heard the sound of water in her shower stall, while she admits taking sponge baths because she hated the shower stalls that always seemed dirty and she having been raised in such a pristine house where everything was spotless due to her grandmother Babu's obsession with cleanliness and order.

Often nervous, tense, and anxious throughout her life, Ramona often wished she could have taken tranquilizers while living with Babu and especially during training. As a result of her anxiety when young and during training, she was somewhat shy, withdrawn, quiet, wanting to please everyone, even though she was seething inside, angry about so many things and angry at so many people, her stress from anger perhaps why she later suffered rheumatoid arthritis and a bi-polar personality disorder similar to her grandmother's.

In addition, her father was often anxious and would pace back and forth when he was waiting on a contract or some other important decision related to his work in film and the theater. During one season of her life, she, too, paced all the time when alone, often to music. During one time when under stress, she paced so much she developed painful sores between her toes that took months to heal.

Reflecting later on her moods, she offered an explanation in typical romantic manner mimicking her father: "I've always been very anxious, my life apparently dominated by the god Apophis an ancient Egyptian deity who embodied chaos as the opponent of light and order and truth and depicted as a giant, golden serpent. I was a very nervous child for too many reasons: My mother very sick with tuberculosis I feared would kill her and eventually did all too soon when I was just entering my teens and the most vulnerable because I knew just enough to understand what was going on in my life. I anxious and fearful while still so young, I felt powerless, locked in the prison of my youth, a time of life when no one understood my numerous fears, my anxieties, my plots to escape from the circumstances that were creating that fear and anxiety and my desire to escape from all those who were crushing my spirit and my will to act on my own trying to resolve my problems while I feared my grandmother more than anyone."

Never openly rebellious to others, Ramona appeared generally quiet and very polite and pleasant because of necessity, partly because of her grandmother, partly because she had grown up with adults, not with noisy siblings, while inwardly, she was a very angry, bitter girl.

When her mother died, friends of Babu meaning well offered their sympathy, but Ramona hated them because they couldn't possibly know how she felt. Later in training, she learned their way of expressing their sympathy was misguided because they offered statements that were trite and inept: "I'm so sorry for your loss," when they had no actual empathy with what she felt.

Always angry at Babu because of the way Babu treated her too often, Ramona was angry at her father because she thought he had deserted her, although eventually she learned why he had been absent for years. Angry at the "system" because a probation officer wanted to take her to Juvenile Hall after her mother died, Ramona refused to go, loudly insisting she wasn't a criminal, just a child who had lost a mother. She frequently was upset because her grandmother and father were always openly fighting each other.

Ramona always angry at the "snooty snotty" girls at L. A. High, especially the Cajun Sorority, including Paula (Ramona's childhood and lifelong friend) who insists that Ramona was liked by members of that society, even inviting her to a sorority outing that Ramona attended, Ramona recalled that when she graduated a year earlier than the rest of her class, she had what she felt the great pleasure of turning down an invitation to join the Cajun Society.

Paula also offers an assessment of her relationship with Ramona: "We met in kindergarten at Wilton Place Elementary School in L.A. and became best friends from then until she went to the Hollywood Professional School around 5th grade. We were born on the same day, Nov. 6, 1935. She lived one block from me and we walked to and from school together. I knew everyone in her family, and she knew everyone in my family as well. After 9th grade, Ramona transferred from Hollywood Professional School to L.A. High School, where again we were the best of friends and walked to and from school every day. After graduating from L.A. High School, we both worked for Farmers Insurance on Wilshire Blvd., and again she and I walked to and from work for a year, when thereafter she went to UCLA and I to Los Angeles City College."

Yet Joan admits she still was angry at Paula after almost 60 years because when they both went to work for Farmers Insurance, Paula was a secretary, i.e. a "big wheel," because she had studied typing and shorthand, while Ramona who had studied Latin and literature and philosophy was a lowly file clerk. How she despised that unbelievably boring job, her fingernails always torn from shoving files into a file drawer. Given all of these experiences, she didn't have contact with Paula for forty years until Paula had actively searched for her after Joan had published her widely used book on medical-surgical nursing.

Paula, in another email, remarked on Joan's accomplishments: "I didn't realize until recently what an important contributor Joan had been to health care because of all the books she wrote. During all the many hours of our phone conversations over several years, she spoke very little about her remarkable capabilities I was well aware of since I was her best friend for her early years before she started nursing school. Her high-achieving school performance, her acting, her piano playing, her poetry, her father having inspired her to become a writer, the loss of her mother who was really her very best friend when Ramona was only around 12 years old, all that played into her becoming the author of those very impressive health books. Of course, I praised her at the time I first learned of them, but now I realize that she deserved even more praise."

When Ramona went into training under the assumed name of Joan Grey, she started to dislike other people besides Babu and for a time her father until they reunited, the only difference, the people she disliked in training all the other students disliked as well, especially the OR nurses and even more so Miss Loftus, the nursing school counselor whom they all despised for just about putting all of them into the psych ward just across the street from their barracks. In fact, Senior class students actually were locked in the psych ward for a whole weekend to grill and observe them for any taint of homosexuality that fueled Miss Loftus' obsession steeped in Freudian psychology's focus on sexual repression.

Joan recalls Miss Loftus sitting stiffly, rarely smiling and even then her smile cold, more a grimace as if she were in pain, always serious, severe in manner, the so-called nursing school counselor Ramona would soon learn had a dominating personality with a cold, clinical side completely lacking in empathy or even sympathy. Equally emphatic were the counselor's views offered as reasons for why students would likely fail the nursing program at County. Her attitude was especially vicious regarding any student suggesting a hint of homosexuality and anyone she thought were using denial to defend themselves from her inquisition. Hating homosexuals, considering them diseased according to the standard medical diagnosis at the time, she would repeatedly offer what became her mantra: "We cannot allow any homosexual to remain in this school! Anyone even suspected of homosexuality should be immediately expelled!"

Besides ridding the world of homosexuals, her main goal seemed to be gaining control over students by forcing them to abandon their defenses, and she too often reached her goal by actually reducing some students to psychic collapse and forcing others to abandon training.

Her own sexual preference appeared strictly heterosexual, but most who had faced her insistent challenges concluded that with her harsh manners and attitudes she most likely would never attract a male for a husband. So along with her strident, passionate campaign against homosexuality, some with sufficient background in psychology surmised her zealous campaign was a reaction to her own tendencies and was transferring her own inclinations onto them her helpless victims to whom she was attracted, an inclination she needed to deny. Her repeated and openly expressed feelings that those whom she supposedly counseled were weak allowed her to easily make them feel guilty. But although considered a villain by most students, she always unwaveringly perceived herself as an excellent, helpful counselor by forcing students to face their "deep-seated" psychic problems, no matter how revealing or painful or self-destructive that confession.

With a degree in psychology she posted on a wall in her office above her desk, she with her facile, destructive form of Freudian psychology and her cold and cruel manner the best way to control her clients, she always believing she was helping them by breaking down their defenses even if other faculty questioned or challenged her methods, she had misused what little she had learned to gain power over them, and too often when she exerted her power, she too often brought some vulnerable student to the brink of mental collapse.

Although Loftus' religious beliefs were never openly stated, her views she sometimes declared with such passion suggested an extreme fundamentalist attitude. Students would often discuss their counselor when at that time they knew nothing about her life or her interests but decided they had to continually defend themselves against someone who always played a zero sum game: if she always had to win, someone would always have to lose. So because of her game skills, too many of them still innocent and ignorant lost their self-esteem. Most of them had problems with her because none of them fit her mold and would never forget her wanting to totally dominate and shape them into an image she approved by systematically and persistently using everything in her power and bag of tricks to break down any defense they could muster. So in the guise of being a helpful counselor believing totally that the duty of the psychologist was to break their denial, she was actually a cruel and vindictive person who wanted to mold them into an image of which she could approve and thus build her own self-esteem until they finally understood that she was a typical bully who enjoyed harassing others to deny, transfer, and thus minimize her own inadequacies.

As a result, the more Ramona met with her, the more confused she became about who she was and whether anything she did was right and honest and normal. So she had to work for too a long time to recover from the damage done. The worse aspect of the situation, no one could openly fight back without risking expulsion, yet another obstacle Ramona had to overcome in addition to all the others with which she had struggled that had prompted Loftus to oppose her being allowed to attend the school of nursing.

Eventually Ramona got away from both her neurotic counselor and her compulsive, abusive grandmother and went on to face other challenges, but by then she had learned how to deal with people who constantly tried to put her down, and she had learned how to fight back and win since as her father used to claim: "Success is the best revenge that is best when eaten cold."

Ramona never did quite understand the "eaten cold" part. She thought "hot" would best express her feelings towards people she disliked because of their attempts to question or belittle her abilities.

Later, through distance and time, Joan readily understood Loftus trying to break students by destroying every defense mechanism had almost succeeded by driving Ramona to the point she didn't know if her choices were typical or born out of some need to deny her problems or a need to transfer her faults onto some other poor soul who had nothing to do with her problems and the issues of how to solve them. "When I finally accepted that I was as normal as any other typical 18-year-old, I decided I could stop allowing this so-called "counselor" to ruin my day while making hers."

As an only child, Ramona at first wasn't at ease with her classmates in training at County. The situation improved when she became close friends with Zan and Linda. "As different as the three of us were, we were like the three musketeers. But I eventually enjoyed many of the other students. A few were much older in their late twenties and early thirties. The men were all former medics during the Korean War, so they were already very experienced and mostly unfazed by some of the horrors we saw and the misery we had to deal with."

While in training, Ramona never indulged in any vices. "I've never smoked or used illegal drugs throughout life. Trying only one puff of nicotine made me so sick, I never tried again, and I so hated the sight of cigarette butts in dirty ashtrays, especially at meals when I lived with Babu and Aunts Jessie and Johnnie and found their smoking such a disgusting habit that I would place glasses on the dining room table so I wouldn't have to look at dirty ashtrays piled with cigarette butts and ashes spilling out onto the crisp, white tablecloth. Babu who was a heavy smoker and messy despite her obsession with cleanliness and order, leaving yucky ashtrays everywhere filled with half-smoked cigarettes, the ends covered with red lipstick, I now surmise our lovely house must have stunk badly from second-hand smoke because almost everybody smoked at the time except me. The one vice I will confess I had during training was cursing, but the only word I used all of us used all the time to describe the actual conditions we endured, and I still sometimes use that word even in my later years when it seems appropriate."

Ramona did very well in training, although she really didn't like the work and often wondered, "Will I ever have a pleasant day when someone doesn't vomit all over me, or I have to clean up feces, or they die on me!" And there was the constant pressure of trying not to admit failure: No student, especially a probationer, could ever say, "I can't do something difficult" because that would show a lack of confidence, an attitude considered a grave sin at Los Angeles County General Hospital School of Nursing and the offender could be summarily expelled.

Yet student nurses were a large part of the labor force for the hospital that would not have managed without their efforts or the dedication of interns and residents all basically working for little pay except the rich experience County provided when "overall employee morale was low, the nursing shortage had not improved, and changes in technology and medical science made greater demands on nursing on a daily basis" [21]. As someone once told her: "If you work at County long enough, you'll see every disease known and some that aren't."

Joan once surmised that generally speaking Ramona had been a compassionate nurse who felt deeply for her patients and went out of her way to try and make them comfortable, an objective nearly impossible to fulfill because they were so many and all so sick or in such pain. No surprise that Ramona did burn out in her Senior year.

"We all did, but I tried not to take my frustrations out on my patients, not like the Senior when I was a Junior and I was helping clean up a woman who had soiled her bed. I remember the Senior saying every word the patient could clearly hear: 'Wait until you've been here another year. You'll hate to clean up these big, fat old bitches as much as I do!'

"I'll never forget the way the patient looked at me totally humiliated.

In the utility room I said to the Senior: 'Why are you still in training? Obviously you hate nursing! You despise the patients! Why don't you just quit?'

She replied with smug assurance: 'It's much too late to quit. But you just wait. You'll be as sick of this place as I am.'

"Yet that student did me a big favor. Whenever I started to feel angry and disgusted with the conditions of the hospital and the patients as well, I just thought about Blondie and that day I put Blondie on my most hated persons list. I made up my mind that I would get out of nursing before I became like her, and I thought that justice would be served if she ended old, sick, poor, and at the mercy of someone as nasty and as uncaring as she."

Ramona always disliked such haughty, arrogant people who looked down on others. "I like people with a healthy sense of humor who make me feel good about myself. I also enjoy people with the same interests as mine, but I also appreciate people who challenge my ideas and help keep my ebbing adrenalin flowing."

Always an excellent student, she excelled in the theoretical aspects of training for being a nurse, but if she could have decided again, she would not have gone into nursing or health care but most likely into play or screenwriting. Babu never wanted her to go into nursing always ranting: "Nursing takes a weak mind and a strong back." Not so true anymore since nursing education has advanced as a result of Joan's textbook, *Medical-surgical Nursing: A Psychophysiological Approach*, once considered by many the "Bible of Nursing.

About her success as a writer, Joan observed, "I always have been very self-disciplined about work. I always have tried to do good work and I almost always meet deadlines. Hard to do when you don't have someone standing right over you all of the time urging you to work.

"I've been blessed with the ability to get up at 4:30 in the morning, one ability that got me through nursing school, although I did sometimes use smelling salts to stay awake in class. My classmates always got a big laugh out of that, and our instructor would stop her lecture to question the hilarity as if we might be laughing at her.

I always could work long hours no matter how tired until I got old. Everything seems to go at once when you get old: your health, your work ethic, your love life. So many losses with age: friends die or move away, children grow up and you now need them instead of they needing you, and you no longer have the respect you once had because young people equate old age with weakness and stupidity."

She claimed to have always been one of the least prejudiced people you will ever meet. However, she did discover when she wrote *Transcultural Communication in Health Care* she didn't like Caucasians nearly as much as other ethnicities. From her perspective, and most likely experience, she found Caucasian men especially greedy, cared little for their families, looked down on women, and were self-centered, her assertions leading to her admitting, "I guess what I just claimed makes me just as prejudiced as others!"

She also claimed, "I'm very glad that I'm not a jealous person. I know people who are tortured by the problem. I've been hurt by a lot by men, but I don't seem to get jealous. In fact, lots of times I have enjoyed my male friend's female friends much more than I liked him. I've always enjoyed the company of women more than men, perhaps because of living as a child in a household of only women, but I can't imagine falling in love with a woman or having sex with one. Perhaps my life would have been easier. But then, upon reflection, maybe not so much when I observe such relationships too often are not loving and actually possessive."

Joan considered Ramona very fortunate to have inherited her father's great talent for writing and, oddly, to receive the calling to be a nurse from Babu who, of course, was more than just a nurse but also a physical therapist, a preacher, and a smart business woman referring to herself as Dr. Grey and Mother Grey and expecting her clients to do the same.

"However angry I was at her or however much I might have disliked what she did to make me miserable during my youth, I have always admired and respected Babu's talents."

During training, my goal was to graduate, become confident and independent, have a close relationship with my dad while making some progress toward getting my Bachelor of Arts degree. During training, my greatest achievement was to make it through the severe stress of being a student at Los Angeles County General Hospital School of Nursing and finally graduating with my diploma and gaining my RN. Those accomplishments gave me the confidence to take on any challenge in nursing and other related challenges such as writing textbooks that were widely used.

I went to night school at East Los Angeles College while in training. I would like to have the boundless energy and ambition that I had during training. My mistake was to go into nursing primarily because I wanted to get away from my grandmother. If I had it to do again, I'd continue teaching and writing in an academic field other than nursing. However, as Uncle Ned pointed out, the most practical thing to do at the time was to go into nursing. It would get me away from my grandmother and give me a secure profession which would allow me to always support myself. For that advice I have been very grateful.

Uncle Ned had researched schools of nursing and encouraged me to go to L.A. County because it provided more experience than any other nursing school, and he certainly was right about that! But what happened to Uncle Ned was tragic and something I will never forget."

I always thought I'd get married eventually, but I never wanted a big wedding like my friend Paula. I got married in Reno with strangers as witnesses. I wanted children, but I didn't want to stay home and just take care of chamacos. I wanted both children and a career. I wanted all of the same choices — every one of them — and all the advantages men have had especially during the '50s, when people insisted that women make a choice: home or career. I felt that men didn't have to make that choice, why should I? So I chose a career."

Boys and men usually liked me a lot. As one male Mexican friend once said: "You are very simpatico," and Rick (my boyfriend while I was in training) thought I was perfect for him. Most men also tended to be very cordial and protective toward me, such as the truckers with whom Linda and I often rode with to escape County for awhile, and I didn't fear the men I should have been afraid of on Jail Ward. I often took chances being around such men by playing billiards with them, but happily I never got hurt.

I always loved men who were very masculine, macho, and good-looking but smart. However, loving and liking a man are very different feelings. The men I dated I didn't really care for as I would a best friend, and I found that too many so-called men lacking mature emotional development only wanted to dominate and possess someone to satisfy their own physical and psychic needs, thus too often warranting the apt label 'boyfriend'.

Now with one marriage and one divorce and former lovers gone, none of my current relationships are 'romantic' since I'm too old. I love pets but couldn't have one in training, had dogs I lost in one way or another, and also a cat or two that seemed to have owned me. When I look back, I guess Uncle Ned was my model for a man I could fall in love with if he hadn't had his terrible drinking problem.

After I fled Babu's house, I soon learned that she was right about nursing being a demanding profession and that I would be much better off doing something else. She knew all about nursing from having started her training when nursing was really crude with multiple responsibilities but no authority and offering no respect. Nurses were considered either maids or morons, angels of mercy or whores who could only perform the most menial tasks. Perhaps I might have done better with a little support from Babu, but nursing did free me from her and from a miserable life in her compulsively strictly-ordered house, and I was able to break free from the tight chains of her possessiveness.

So what if I had to empty bedpans and make beds, and defer to doctors who were not nearly as bright as I was. At least nursing provided a clear way out and a clear path ahead; at least I'd be able to support myself and tell anyone who tried to stop me or control me to get lost. At least nursing offered me some degree of power; at least it gave me a secure place in the world; at least becoming a nurse and going through training proved that I had fortitude even though people didn't believe I had brains.

Babu always maintained I was smart enough to become anything I wanted to be. Sadly, what she claimed wasn't quite true. I was terrific at understanding literary theory and sociological concepts but horrible at math and physics. With my SATs in the top 2% of students in written and verbal skills and in the bottom 2% in mechanical skills, I now wonder how I got into nursing school, let alone completing training since nursing required an ability to perform complex procedures and determine medication dosages, both I had to really work at. But I readily understood anatomy and physiology and psychology. So these unequal abilities balanced out in the end and I was able to graduate and practice my profession. I wanted to graduate from nursing school and go on to the university and get my degree in philosophy and literature or some other program not related to nursing. I didn't appreciate nursing other than as a means to get away from Babu whom I actually disliked because of all the hurt and grief she caused me with her constant criticisms and her abusive behavior when I was still young enough for her to get away with it. Now she would most likely be charged with child abuse.

When I graduated, nursing would still just be a means to an end for earning enough money to buy the necessities of life while I pursued more 'intellectual' and creative avenues that probably wouldn't bring me any money for a long time. I wanted to become a screenwriter like my dad, but he said I should write books instead.

Dad was an "idea man" and he would give me ideas that he urged me to develop. Dad warned me that screenwriting and working in Hollywood was a brutal business that brought mostly disappointment and eventually anger and bitterness from a system becoming always more in-grown shutting out anyone who wasn't already connected to someone prominent within that system.

'Write a book and let the studios come to you!' Dad advised instead. 'Then you'll have a chance to become a screenwriter. But remember even if your life may be rosy for a while, working for Hollywood eventually will go sour and end badly. Writing is not like nursing where you know that if you work hard you'll always have a job. Writing screenplays or even books is like playing the horses. No matter how much you learn about the horses in the race, you always only have a slight chance you might win if some horse suddenly appears from nowhere and runs wonderfully and brings you reward. But there are no assurances! None! Especially in Hollywood! You might win for a while, but unless you're very lucky, you'll start losing and it will be all down hill from there. Even if you win at writing, you should stick to nursing. Keep those skills you learned as a backup. You're going to need them because a streak of luck is just that – a flash on the screen, a dream that's eventually going to end and you wake up to the real world of hard knocks!'

I always knew Dad was right about the too often harsh reality of the actual world. The odd characteristic about Dad, he was also an optimist. Despite rejections and problems in his life, Dad just kept on working every day and often all night. He loved writing; he loved his characters; he loved playing god controlling and directing their action. So success and money were important because he also had to live in the actual, everyday world, but not as important as his work that came first before everything else, including me.

Yet I didn't totally accept Dad's advice that I shouldn't try writing what I wanted to write. While training to become a nurse, I saw enough characters, enough scenes played out on the hospital stage to give me enough ideas for a lifetime of writing. I didn't immediately appreciate nursing because of the constant demands, the unrelenting pressure, the ugly situations we had to deal with everyday. I, too often, would think: 'Will I ever have a day when someone doesn't vomit all over me or suffer pain that I can't relieve, or I have to deal with a doctor or head nurse who isn't yelling at me because of some incident I couldn't handle because of my inexperience!' And, of course, I recall Aunt Jessie's wise remark while on my way to County to begin three years of rigorous training that I would always have someone yelling at me throughout my life.

Writing surely would have years of disappointment with few if not rare moments of success, but at least I would be following my own path even if I could never completely isolate myself from much of the ugliness in the world. Free to think and act as I wanted even if my efforts didn't bring success and fame, at least I would have as much freedom as I would ever have. My father had obstacles he too often created for himself, but at least he was free to follow his beliefs and write about what he felt was important. I, instead, found I was never free in nursing because I felt bound by rules and confined by traditions based on nurses being little more than servants and women in general no more respected than the family pet. But the two things I wanted most was the security that nursing brings and the freedom that writing offers.

In addition to the persistent probing of the nursing school counselor, or most likely because of her, I went through a period of extreme burnout early in my Senior year. Yet as tired as I felt, I found all patients compelling, not just their diseases. Their lives and experiences varied so wildly. I witnessed families who either cared about them and were there for them or had dumped them and had forgotten them as they pursued their own lives. So even though we in training were as poor as so many of our patients, in many ways we were rich from all we were learning about people, diseases, procedures, surgeries, and mental illness. And we knew that our knowledge and experience would pay us well and prepare us for carrying out our profession anywhere in the world throughout our lives.

Nursing students who had graduated from the less demanding and more academic schools were probably always a bit afraid of the working world of nursing at County because they most likely lacked the firm confidence and fearlessness that had been infused into us during our three years of training where I too often saw too many people die, their deaths taking many forms: Some died in pain that only the strongest narcotics could ease. Others died in a coma, these poor people already dead, their heart rhythm still recorded by a machine, brain waves still running out on paper until the machine finally records only flatline responses and some nurse or doctor turns it off. Some died surrounded by family and friends feeling grief, sobbing over the loss that is coming and knowing that death is so final, so permanent. Sometimes a priest or minister or rabbi at the patient's bedside administered last rites and claiming the patient will be going to some sacred place none of us have ever seen, the family's grief sometimes relieved by these words but at other times feeling even worse at their loss and dreaming of when they would be united with their loved ones.

I saw so many others die alone without friends, family, or spiritual guide at their bedside. No one held their hand or smoothed back their hair or told them that they will be going to a better place. These, the very poor, the derelict, the homeless without family would be going to the county crematorium where what was once a living body would burn to ashes buried in some landfill. A priest, a rabbi, a minister might be there to preach some words of empty hope and promise although nobody would be listening, no one would be there to hear those words and feel some small comfort.

I have learned that all deaths are a loss. Death from an illness, an accident, or simply old age represent a life that is gone and unless remembered will likely be forgotten by children, parents, or by the people they loved who will also die taking the memory of their loved one with them. All deaths are sad, but the saddest death of all is the death that could have been prevented. A life needlessly lost, who knows what that person would have done if only she or he had lived.

I often think of how my mother's unnecessary death completely changed my life as well as my grandmother's life and my father's life. I know from the moment I saw that my mother was dead I was never the same. The loss of my mother left me emotionally scarred for life. And I am still so sensitive to that loss I can spot a motherless child without knowing the person or anything about her. I sense their sadness that I can feel it myself, and sometimes I feel anger that has been long buried. These emotions didn't stop me from succeeding as a nurse but made me more sensitive to others and their too often needless suffering.

So sometimes when I have felt envious of other people's appearance, their seemingly more fortunate lives, or their wealth, I would ask myself: "While I might enjoy some aspects of a person's life, would I really want to live with all aspects of her life: Bad marriages or relationships with abusive or alcoholic men or both, problems dealing with people for whom I care abusing alcohol or other drugs, abusive parents, disrespectful or abusive children, predatory friends scheming to get my hard-earned wealth? My answer has always been, NO! For I unfortunately have too frequently already fully enjoyed all those experiences."

Endnotes

[1] Cover photo:

Title: [Los Angeles County General Hospital exterior] (3 views)

Date: [ca. 1933]

Collection: California History Section Picture Catalog

Owning Institution: California State Library

Source: Calisphere

Date of access: April 25 2018 13:47

[2] See https://en.wikipedia.org/wiki/Gloria_Grey

[3] Courtesy Library of Congress.

Grogan, Brian, "ALTERNATE SITE VIEW OF CESAR CHAVEZ BRIDGE LOOKING NORTHEAST. - Macy Street Viaduct, Los Angeles, Los Angeles County, CA." Library of Congress Prints and Photographs Division (HAER CA-277-5. Accessed April 29, 2018).

[4] Los Angeles County General Hospital exterior] (3 views)

Date: 1932

Collection: California History Section Picture Catalog

Owning Institution: California State Library

Source: Calisphere

Date of access: April 25, 2018

[5] Los Angeles County General Hospital exterior] (3 views)

Date: 1932

Collection: California History Section Picture Catalog

Owning Institution: California State Library

Source: Calisphere

Date of access: April 25, 2018

18 13:38

[6] See Martin, History, (p.115); *Looking Back*, (p.156).

[7] *Looking Back*, (p.151).

[8] *Looking Back*, (p.151)

[9] *RX 1957*, (p.16)

[10] Looking Back, (p.156-157)

[11] *California and Western Journal,* Vol XL, No 6, p. 477, June 1934

[12] See again https://en.wikipedia.org/wiki/Gloria_Grey

[13] Los Angeles County General Hospital exterior] (3 views)

Date: 1932

Collection: California History Section Picture Catalog

Owning Institution: California State Library

Source: Calisphere

Date of access: April 25, 2018

[14] Courtesy Library of Congress.

Grogan, Brian, "PART 2 OF 3 PART PANORAMA OF FOURTH STREET VIADUCT WITH NOS. CA-280-1 AND CA-280-3. LOOKING NORTH. - Fourth Street Viaduct, Spanning Los Angeles River, Los Angeles, Los Angeles County, CA" (HAER CA-280-2. Accessed April 29, 2018).

[15] *Looking Back*, (p.159).

[16] *Rx 1957* Yearbook, (p.92).

[17] *Rx 1957* Yearbook, (pp. 90-91).

[18] *Looking Back*, (p.164).

[19] Paula Strahm E-mail to LACSON Alumni Association. High school photo of Ramona courtesy of Paula Shram.

[20] E-mail to LACSON Alumni Association.

[21] *Looking Back*, (p.158).

Sources

A Century of Distinction. 1895-1995. DVD (43 min). Los Angeles County College of Nursing & Allied Health.

California and Western Journal, Vol XL, No 6, p. 477, June,1934

Library of Congress Prints and Photographs Division.

Looking Back—A Century of Nursing: The History of the Los Angeles County Medical Center School of Nursing 1895-1995. Sunland, California, Ty Wood Printing, 2000. (pp.156-158, 164).

Los Angeles County General Hospital - Google Search LAC+USC Medical Center

Martin, Helen Eastman, M. D. *The History of the Los Angeles County Hospital* (1878-1968). Los Angeles, University of Southern California Press, 1979. (p.115).

RX 1957. Annual Publication of the Student Body—Los Angeles County General Hospital—School of Nursing. Ralph George, Editor. (pp.16, 90-92).

Wikipedia. Los Angeles General Hospital v.II - a gallery on Flickr
https://en.wikipedia.org/wiki/
LAC%2BUSC_Medical_Center:https://www.kcet.org/shows/
visiting-with-huell-howser/episodes/county-usc-medical-center
http://articles.latimes.com/2008/oct/27/opinion/oe-eckstein27
http://yamashirohollywood.com/about/yamashirohistory/[1]
https://en.wikipedia.org/wiki/Gloria_Grey
https://en.wikipedia.org/wiki/Natalie_Wood

---

1.   http://yamashirohollywood.com/about/yamashiro

Acknowledgments

Joan Kohl, MSN, BSN, RN, Dean, School of Nursing for providing source materials and forwarding emails from Paula Strahm as well as providing Paula Strahm's email address.

Karen Luckmann for providing first-hand information of her mother's later years and final days, as well as providing family photos that I had never seen.

Paula Strahm for frequent exchanges of emails answering my questions and confirming the information I had received from Karen Luckmann.